THE POMEGRANATE TREE

A MEMOIR

ALIZA ELLINS

Paperback ISBN: 979-8-9912197-2-3

Ebook ISBN: 979-8-3306242-6-3

CONTENTS

In the heart of life's storm, stands the Pomegranate Tree,
Roots deep in the earth, reaching for eternity.
A symbol of resilience, of strength through the years,
A testament to love, and overcoming fears.

Its branches tell stories of family and love,
Of generations past, watching from above.
Through challenges faced, it stands tall and true,
A reminder that in darkness, light shines through.

With each scar on its bark, a lesson learned,
Each tear shed for growth; each flame burned.
It teaches of dedication, of hard work and strife,
Of never giving up, even in the darkest night.

In its shade, find solace and peace,
In its fruit, a taste of sweetness never to cease.
Embrace yourself, as the Pomegranate Tree does,
For in self-love lies strength, in oneself, one trusts.

In the Jewish faith, it's a symbol of life,

Each seed a promise, amidst turmoil and strife.
So, stand tall like the Pomegranate Tree,
For in resilience and love, lies the key.

INTRODUCTION

 "From generation to generation; לְדוֹר וָדוֹר; L'dor Vador"

— *PSALM 10:6*

WHY THE POMEGRANATE

Pomegranates have deep roots in history, often mentioned in the Torah in verses like Exodus 28:33-35, 1 Kings 7:20, 2 Kings 25:17, Jeremiah 52:22-23, Isaiah 46:9-11, Numbers 13:23, Deuteronomy 8:8, and the Song of Solomon 6:11, 7:12, 8:2. In ancient times, the presence of pomegranate trees symbolized a nation's wealth and prosperity. In Jewish traditions taught that the pomegranate's 613 seeds correspond to the 613 mitzvot, or commandments, in the Torah. Others see the pomegranate as a symbol of Israel, representing the sweet abundance that the Promised Land offers. My book, this journey you're holding, is no accident—just as pomegranates have been an essential part of my life by no mere coincidence.

In my life, the pomegranate has become a meaningful symbol, representing the joys and challenges I've faced along the way. It connects me to Tunisia, where my mother was born, and where the rich soil nurtured the first pomegranates. A vibrant pomegranate tree in Israel witnessed the challenges of my childhood, its blossoms and vibrant fruits reflect the strength that grew within me. The ancient city of Carthage in Tunisia, known for cultivating this unique fruit, is more than just a place on the map—it's a chapter in the cultural and historical significance of the pomegranate that shaped who I am.

Today, as I stand in my family home, surrounded by the laughter of my children, grandchildren, and friends, another flourishing pomegranate tree stands nearby. It's a living reminder of the history shared between this fruit and my family. This tree links past and present; bringing warmth and life into the walls that sheltered me during my formative years. As my family gathers beneath its branches, in our family home, we're reminded of our journey from challenges to triumphs, with each leaf and juicy pomegranate telling a story of perseverance.

The pomegranate is more than just a fruit; it's a symbol that connects me to my past and guides me into the future. As a Jewish woman, the concept of "L'dor V'dor," from generation to generation, is deeply meaningful to me. This memoir, "The Pomegranate Tree," is not just a recounting of my life; it's a reflection of the strength that has shaped me and continues to guide my journey.

Rooted in historical trade routes and cultural exchanges, the pomegranate holds a special place in the hearts of Tunisians. Its vibrant color and unique flavor made it a staple in local cuisine and a symbol of prosperity and abundance. The fruit's journey from the arid landscapes of North Africa to the Promised Land of Israel reflects the determination of the people who cultivated it, nurturing a symbol that transcends borders and time. To me, the pomegranate takes on an even deeper meaning, echoing the ancient wisdom of the Torah. Much like its 613 seeds, each representing commandments and virtuous deeds, my life and my family's story reflect a life shaped by strength, joy, and a lasting legacy of lives well-lived.

As I think about the significance of the pomegranate, I'm moved by the realization that its roots are intertwined with the very roots of my family. Originating from Tunisia, just like my beloved mother, the pomegranate becomes more than a symbol—it's a living testament to the strong roots of love and beauty that bind me across generations and across the world.

The Pomegranate Tree holds immense importance to me and my family. From the very beginning of my life, it was there, with roots that run deep into my soul, just like the tree that now stands outside our front door—the home where I have raised my children and grandchildren.

As I consider the significance of the pomegranate, I am filled with gratitude for the strong roots of love and beauty that bind me to my past and guide me into the future. This memoir is my attempt to come to terms with my own trauma and share my stories with my family, my children, and my grandchildren. I hope that through these pages, they will see not just my story, but the story of a people who have faced challenges together, bound by a shared history and a shared belief in the power of perseverance.

The pomegranate's journey from Tunisia to Israel to America mirrors my own—a journey marked by challenges and triumphs. Its vibrant color and unique flavor are a testament to the strength of the human spirit, a spirit that refuses to be bound by borders or constrained by time.

DESIGNING MY LIFE

I am a self-taught individual with an insatiable thirst for knowledge, especially in history. To me, history isn't just about the past; it's the world. I'm also deeply passionate about the art of interior and exterior design —they are expressions of our culture and history, reflecting the essence of whom we are and where we are headed. Through my travels, both near and far, I seek to immerse myself in different cultures, learning from the people I meet and the places I visit.

As I dive into the history of each country I visit, I am struck by the role its people have played in shaping the world today. Their contributions to society, art, and fashion tell a story of creativity, determination, and the enduring human spirit. This passion for understanding and learning from the past fuels my drive to make a meaningful impact. I believe that by understanding where we come from, we can better navigate today's challenges and create a brighter future for tomorrow.

My journey has taught me that it is never too late to pursue your passions and dreams. I've learned to embrace who I am and recognize my own self-worth. This discovery has given me the confidence to go after what truly matters to me and pursue my passions with energy and determination. Through it all, I've found a deep sense of happiness and fulfillment in knowing that I am living authentically, true to myself and my core values.

The lesson I've learned is this: know your worth, pursue your passions, and never stop learning and evolving. Life is a journey, and it's up to us to make the most of it. Embrace who you are, follow your heart, and you will find happiness and gratification beyond measure.

CHAPTER ONE

A MOTHER'S LEGACY: MY MOM'S STORIES

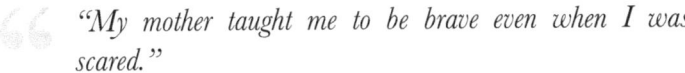

"*My mother taught me to be brave even when I was scared.*"

— GLORIA ESTEFAN

MOM, GERMAINE NEDJMA

As I look back on my mother's life, I'm struck by the loneliness she must have felt as a young girl —the sense of being unloved and unseen. Yet, still in her quiet strength, I find hope—a reminder that even in the darkest times, love has the power to guide us forward.

My Mom

Germaine, my mother, was born in a Jewish ghetto in Tunis Tunisia, December 15, 1932 here her family made a life amid scarcity and hardship. Their home was small, just two rooms in a three-floor walkup tenement. The courtyard's communal well provided water, adding a bit of normalcy to their lives, while the shared kitchen and bathrooms created a hectic community among her family and neighbors. On Fridays and holidays, they would go to the local bathhouse, a Hamman, for a cherished shower—a ritual that was part of the Sabbath and Jewish holidays for generations before them.

Germaine attended a French Jewish school at the local synagogue. When the Holocaust advanced into North Africa and the Germans invaded her hometown of Tunis, she was just ten years old. Standing on her rooftop terrace, she watched in terror as smoke clouded the sky, and screams and cries filled the air. The world momentarily went silent when a German plane, shot down by an Allied aircraft, came crashing into view, hurling toward her. It crashed mere yards from her home, with smoke billowing from the wreckage—a memory that would never leave her. Those dark days became etched into her being.

Soon, the Nazi regime took control, and her family was forced to live in a ghetto. They had to share a room with another family, crammed together with barely any space. Food was scarce, often nonexistent. The family received limited rations, and Germaine and her sister, my Aunt Helen, were tasked with collecting them. They had to become clever and resourceful, learning how to sneak extra food beyond their rations to feed their family. Leaving the ghetto was not allowed; those who did were packed into small transports by soldiers and sent straight to work camps. There, they worked long hours sewing uniforms for Nazi soldiers. Afterward, they were thrown back into the transports and returned directly to the ghetto.

As the war raged, my grandparents sent Germaine and my Aunt Helen to a monastery deep in the French countryside, where the nuns hid them from the Nazis. Germaine told me stories of how much she hated the monastery. She was assigned to do the laundry, spending her days in the hot, muggy laundry room, cleaning boys' clothing amid sweat and steam. Germaine often felt alone and isolated in a place where she felt out of place, as though she no longer had a real home. During their time there, Germaine was known for being shy and meek, while her older sister, my Aunt Helen, took on the role of protector for both of them. Yet, despite everything, her spirit remained strong, embodying the perseverance of our people.

When the war ended and the German army surrendered, there was a glimmer of hope. In 1948, after Israel gained independence, my mother's family boarded a ship to the Promised Land, Israel, leaving behind the horrors of the past to seek a brighter future. When Germaine arrived in Israel, she was sent to a refugee camp. White tents lined the camp, and she was separated from her parents, living in the teenage section. Here, she would finally experience peace, serenity, joy, and freedom. Her time in the camp would come to be described as the best of her life. They worked in the orange groves of Hadera nestled in the northern Sharon Valley of Israel, a task she loved. Surrounded by the sweet citrus scent, she occasionally sneaked a bite, savoring not only the fruit but also a taste of freedom and joy. Laughter echoed through the grove, creating a true sense of happiness. The sky was bright, and the sun shone with a joyous light that Germaine and the other refugees had never thought they would see. The hallmark of Judaism is community, and it was vividly evident here. For the first time, Germaine felt camaraderie and friendship among people her age who were going through similar experiences. They were finally home—a place no one would ever force them to leave, a home that would always accept and welcome them.

At night, they gathered as a community, lively compared to their past lives. There was music, joy, and love. Germaine had nothing material, and sometimes food was hard to come by, but for the first time in her life, she had no worries. She had friends, love, laughter, and a home. Although not all refugees spoke the same language and communication was sometimes difficult, their eyes sparkled with joy for the future they had never expected. There was a universal understanding: they were home, and this was family.

My parents' love story began with a chance introduction arranged by Germaine's older sister, Helen. My father, Emilio, a vibrant and charming eighteen-year-old from Greece, had also migrated with his family from Tunisia to Israel. Their paths crossed in the orange groves, leading them to one of the community gatherings. My mother and father danced together, laughing and smiling, simply enjoying each other's company and having fun.

At just seventeen, my mother was captivated by my father's charm. Their bond grew quickly, leading to a whirlwind marriage a year later. However, their relationship soon turned from passion to heartache, lasting only three months. Unbeknownst to my mother when she made the difficult decision to leave her marital home and my father, she was pregnant with me. Upon discovering this, she chose not to look back and sought comfort in the arms of her parents instead of returning to my father. I was born in Haifa, Israel later that year (1952), the same town where my father would eventually start a new family and raise twelve children. Meanwhile, my mother, ever resourceful, found work as a nurse assistant at the historic mental hospital of Acco, a building that had once served as a British prison. This resourcefulness became a defining trait, helping her keep our family safe and provided for to the best of her abilities.

For the first two years of my life, we lived with my grandparents, who provided unwavering care and affection while my mother worked. As the eldest of four children, I naturally became her anchor—a source of support through both the

4

financial struggles and emotional challenges she faced. Despite her dedication, my mother carried the scars of a difficult upbringing, often grappling with insecurity and doubt. I vividly remember her ask "What will become of me as I grow older?" It was a question that weighed heavily on her, and I always promised her that I would always be by her side and always take care of her.

In her later years, Parkinson's and dementia began to take hold. It was then my turn to fulfill the promise I made in my childhood and take care of her. It was a difficult transition for our entire family, watching her once sharp mind and vibrant spirit fade. Yet, through it all, she was surrounded by love—cherished and cared for until the very end. As I reflect on the moments we shared, both joyful and challenging, one thing remains constant: the love I have for my mother. Despite the demands of my own life, I never lost sight of the fact that she, too, was growing older, her needs changing with time. Although the end was hard, the bond between us remained strong—a testament to the power of a mother's love.

REMEMBERING MY MOM

My Mom

My mother instilled in me a sense of independence and strength that has shaped who I am today. Though she wasn't one for outward displays of affection, her love was undeniable. Even though she didn't receive much emotional support from her own mother or grandmother, I always knew she cherished me deeply. She spoke of me with pride, celebrating my accomplishments as if they were her own. Not a day goes by that I don't miss her. Her wisdom and guidance have been a guiding light in my life, and I've passed on the valuable lessons she taught me to my own children and grandchildren. Her legacy of empathy and unconditional love continues to inspire me as I navigate life's challenges.

Together, my mother and I embarked on many journeys, exploring Europe, North Africa, and the Middle East. These trips weren't just about seeing new places; they were about enriching our lives and creating lasting memories together. Each journey was a celebration of the bond we shared and the joy we found in each other's company. One day, as I drove into town, my thoughts drifted to my dear mother, who had passed away eight years earlier. A wave of sadness washed over me, and I found myself seeking comfort in a local thrift shop. There, amidst the eclectic array of goods, my eyes were drawn to an exquisite 1960s vintage box adorned with ornate jewels.

The inlaid stones—Laborite, turquoise, jasper, jade, agate, apatite, hematite, and peridot (my birthstone)—captivated me. This box, I later learned, was a traditional North African wedding gift, symbolizing love and positive energy for the bride's new home. It held even greater significance for me, as my mother was from Tunisia, North

Bejeweled Box

Africa, and had shared with me the rich traditions of her heritage. I know this box is a gift from my mom, a way for her to remind me that she's gone but always with me. It felt like a twist of fate that this beautiful box had found its way from North Africa to my small town in the Sierra Nevada Foothills of California. Its journey resonated with me, a tangible connection to my roots and a reminder of the stories my mother had shared with me.

I purchased the box with gratitude, knowing it would be cherished and passed down through generations in my family. Now, prominently displayed in our home, it serves as a link to the past and a testament to the power of love and tradition. Reflecting on this unexpected discovery, I couldn't help but think of the significance of gemstones throughout history. With ninety-nine verses about gemstones in the Torah, they have long been a source of fascination, symbolizing not only beauty but also value and energy—a connection that transcends time and culture.

Looking back on my mother Germaine's journey from Tunisia, North Africa, I see a story of perseverance amidst adversity. Born into a poor Jewish family, she experienced loss early in life, surrounded by the echoes of siblings who died at birth and in adolescence. In the cramped quarters of the Jewish ghetto, our family made a life despite the challenges. Yet, amidst the struggles, there was a strong sense of determination. My mother's quiet strength carried us through, her love shining even in the darkest times. As I trace her footsteps through the past, I'm reminded of her unwavering resolve and her deep longing for connection that went beyond our physical hardships. In her, I find not only a mother but a source of hope—a reminder that loves has no boundaries, the power to light even the darkest paths.

SAYING GOODBYE TO MY MOM

So many memories, happily, spend the day browsing around vintage stores for treasure. On this particular day, she was radiant in her favorite white pants and a vibrant colorful flowered top, her enthusiasm for our adventures shining through. Her love for fashion was infectious, and I inherited that from her. She had a petite frame and loved bright colors, with a knack for mixing styles that always caught the eye of strangers who always complimented her. She wore her outfits with such confidence and grace, embodying a beauty that went far beyond her appearance

In one of my errands to Home Depot took an unexpected turn when she needed to use the restroom. Within moments, I heard her call my name. Rushing to her side, I found her trying to clean her stained and soiled white pants and undergarments in the sink, a look of distress on her face. I did my best to calm her, reassuring her that it was just an accident, and everything would be okay. But deep down, I knew that this moment was just a small part of something bigger. Little did I know it would be one of our last outings together?

As my mom stood there, fragile and vulnerable, I knew I had to act quickly. Closing the bathroom door behind me, I raced to find help. The store manager, sensing the urgency in my voice, didn't hesitate to offer assistance. He handed me a thick fabric cover to wrap around my mom's small frame, protecting her privacy and dignity as we quickly exited the store. Back home, the warm water soothed her tired body. The suds washed away the strong odor and scent, and I saw tears streaming down her face. It broke my heart to see her anguish and embarrassment, but I knew I had to stay strong for her.

As I tucked her into bed, her exhaustion evident, I couldn't help but feel grateful for the moments we shared. Despite our live challenging past, I knew that our love overcame all. I hoped that one day my own children would show me the same compassion and care, understanding the depth of maternal love and sacrifice. As I watched her drift off to sleep, I realized that the bond between a mother and child is truly priceless. It's a bond that withstands the test of time, overcoming pain and hardship, leaving a lasting mark on our hearts.

Parkinson's and dementia had taken their toll on my mom, and this moment marked the beginning of the end. Despite the hardships we faced, I always loved and respected her. She deserved nothing less than the utmost care, love, and dignity.

As I reflect on that day, I am reminded of the strength my mom exhibited, even in the face of embarrassment and misfortune. Her unwavering love and optimism continue to guide me. I miss her more than words can express, but I take comfort in the memories we shared and the lessons she taught me about grace, dignity, and the power of a mother's love. The day I lost my mom was the most excruciating and difficult of my life.

My memories of her are deeply profound and there are countless, ensuring she remains with me. Throughout our family's journey, we shared a clear understanding of the challenges we faced together, leaning on each other for support and finding comfort in our shared experiences. But for my mother Germaine, there was a deeper ache—a longing for connection and belonging that transcended our physical hardships.

CHAPTER TWO
SAFTA'S KITCHEN

"The ache for home lives in all of us, the safe place where we can go as we are and not be questioned."

— *MAYA ANGELOU*

MATERNAL GRANDMOTHER, LOUISE

I've been told that as a baby I was very much loved and dotted on. As a child and into my pre-teens it somehow it changed. I longed for the warmth of my grandmother's embrace, but it always seemed just out of reach. I vividly remember one day when I saw her walking down the street near our home Israel. She was impeccably dressed, her makeup flawless, and her smile was warm and inviting. Yet, something felt awkward, I was seven years old I would call out to her, using the affectionate term "Safta" grandma in Hebrew, hoping to get her attention. But her response was distant, her mind somewhere else. When I asked her where she was going, she would simply reply "errands" and continue on her way, leaving me feeling hurt and distanced from the grandmotherly love I craved. I dreamed that she would be present giving us the security that we needed badly while my mom worked.

It seemed my grandmother struggled to connect with me on being the loving, supportive maternal figure. There were no tender moments or comforting hugs when I needed them most, the scars of her emotional distance remained, reminding me of the love I missed out on as a child. It's a pain that still lingers—a longing for the grandmother I wished I had.

Reflecting on those early years, I realize how important it is to nurture relationships and provide emotional support, especially to children and grandchildren. My grandmother's inability to do so left a void in me, a longing for the love and security that only a grandmother's embrace can provide. It's a lesson I carry with me as I strive to be the loving presence I never had with my own grandchildren.

But as we moved away and settled into our own home, that sense of attachment and belonging gradually faded. Despite living nearby, visits from my grandparents became very rare, and at a young age, I felt the emptiness of their absence. It wasn't until my grandmother's later years that I felt that love and connection return. Even though she struggled with English after five decades in America, she spoke to me in a mix of Arabic, French, and Hebrew. We all learned to communicate in our own way, relying on patience and understanding to bridge the gaps.

In those moments, I found a real sense of connection that went beyond language. It felt like her love and wisdom reached me through her gestures and the way she carried herself, making me feel closer to her despite the barriers. Still, there was a bittersweet realization that time had taken its toll on our relationship, leaving us with only a few moments to truly connect. Even so, I cherished those moments, appreciating the warmth of her love and the time we spent together. I knew that she really loved me and was very proud of my all accomplishments.

Our family gatherings, whether in Israel or the United States, became cherished traditions. The long table, filled with delicious North African dishes prepared by my grandmother and mother, was the heart of our holidays. The aroma of spices filled the air, and every bite of food connected us to our heritage—a testament to my grandmother's cooking and her deep love for family. Among all the dishes, the chicken soup with couscous held a special place in my heart. It wasn't just a meal; it was a symbol of love and tradition, one that I have carried on with my own family. I now cook those same recipes, sharing the love and tradition with my grandchildren. But even as I watched her in the kitchen, pouring care into every dish, I couldn't help but feel a longing for something more—an emotional connection that always seemed just out of reach.

Whenever my grandmother visited us at our home on Crescent Heights, she would open her handbag and pull out candies and Chiclets gum, offering them with a warm smile. Married for over sixty years, my grandparents shared a deep bond, though they had their disagreements like any couple. My Safta was known for her frugality; she was incredibly careful with her money, never wasting a penny. This carefulness stemmed from the poverty she experienced in her lifetime, and she always wanted to ensure she had something left over. Despite her frugality, when she passed away, I discovered an envelope full of cash in her nightstand—an unexpected find that contrasted with her usual carefulness with money. It reminded me of her generosity, not just in material things but in preserving our family's North African heritage. She also had a practical side; she would give me money for groceries and insist I bring back the receipt and change. Her childhood struggles had shaped her, and through this, I learned compassion and understanding for the people who raised me.

The relationship between my mother and grandmother

highlights the complexities of our family dynamics. My mother at times was frustrated by the attention given to her brothers, while my grandmother seemed unaware of the emotional impact of her actions. It created a silent rift that echoed through the generations, with the men in our family always being held to different standards than the women. It was a cycle of emotional distance that I was determined to break.

As the eldest of four children, I saw firsthand the effects of this generational trauma on my siblings and me. Yet, despite the turmoil, I found strength in my love for them, becoming a source of support during tough times. Our childhood was marked by challenges, but it was also a journey of growth—a testament to the power of love and determination. Looking back, I realize the importance of breaking free from the past, leading with empathy, understanding, and forgiveness. It's a lesson I carry with me as I strive to create a loving, accepting home for my own children and grandchildren.

As my grandmother's health declined rapidly, our bond grew stronger. I often visited her in the afternoons, listening to our favorite Arabic songs on an old creaky record player. The music by Farid El Attarch, a renowned Egyptian singer, brought back memories of her life in Tunisia. When she passed away, it felt like our families light had dimmed. The foundation around which our family revolved was no longer there, and she was only with us in spirit. In the years that followed, my extended family began to drift apart. Some of us,

My Paternal Grandparents

14

including myself, moved to different cities, making it harder to maintain the closeness we once shared. But despite the physical distance, we worked to keep our family bonds strong, coming together for special occasions and cherishing the memories of those who had passed.

In the end, it's these simple, meaningful moments that remind me of the enduring power of love. Even though our time together was brief, the love we shared will always be a part of me, a testament to the bonds of family and the strength of the human spirit.

MATERNAL GRANDFATHER, MOSHE (MOISE)

My grandfather was born in Libya, and not much is known about his early childhood. He moved to Tunisia with his single mother and sister, and later married my grandmother Louise. Together, they had nine children, though only five survived to adulthood.

One of my earliest memories is of my fifth birthday, celebrated in my grandparents' backyard. It was a warm, joyful day, with laughter and the scent of freshly cut grass in the air. I was their second oldest grandchild, and I basked in the attention. The party was full of happiness, with trays of candy laid out for everyone. But as the day came to an end, something happened that clouded my happiness.

My grandfather, usually a calm and wise man, became upset when the children began to take the candy home. In his frustration, he asked them to put them back in the tray, unaware of how disappointed I was. It was a small moment, but it felt like a crack in the perfection of my special day. Despite this, my love for my grandfather never wavered. We shared many moments of laughter and storytelling, and I was fascinated by his tales of life in Tunisia, which gave me a deep connection to our history and heritage.

He was a tailor by trade, skilled in turning fabric into

beautiful and functional garments. During the war, he had to sew uniforms for the soldiers who were occupying his home-land—a necessary sacrifice for survival. I treasured our time together, especially our walks through downtown Los Ange-les's garment district, where he would point out the differences in the quality of the fabric with the expertise of someone who had spent years in the craft. Health and not His blindness in one eye was a reminder of the hardships he had faced, but he never let it slow him down when he got older, not going to frequent checkups illness began to creep in. Prostate cancer slowly took away his strength, and though he rarely saw doctors—perhaps out of fear or stubbornness—it was a choice that ultimately cost him his life. His passing left a deep void in our family, and we mourned him with heavy hearts. But even in our grief, there was a lesson: the importance of cherishing every moment.

In his memory, my daughter was given the scissors that had been his tool of trade. They were a symbol of his hard work and strength, a reminder that love and hope can endure even in the face of adversity. As I look back on the moments we shared, I am grateful for the lessons he taught me, the love he gave me, and the legacy he left behind. I think of my grandparents always with so much love and admiration.

Surrounded by these memories, I feel deeply connected to my roots. My grandfather's lessons became my own, weaving together a story of love, heritage, and resilience. Their home was a sanctuary, a place where time seemed to stand still, allowing me to savor every precious moment with them.

CHAPTER THREE

GENERATIONAL RESILIENCE

> *"The legacy of heroes is the memory of a great name and the inheritance of a great example."*
>
> — *BENJAMIN DISRAELI*

AUNT HELEN

In the presence of Aunt Helen, I always felt a sense of awe. She wasn't just an aunt; she was a beacon of strength, wisdom, and boundless energy. To me, she was the original influencer—a pillar of guidance whose presence inspired everyone around her to reach for their dreams. Her aura was magnetic, drawing people in with her unwavering confidence and warmth.

Aunt Helen

Growing up, Aunt Helen's dynamic personality left an significant mark on my impressionable mind. Despite the constant demands of her bustling household and the pressures of a thriving career in real estate, she always made time for us. I vividly remember the sound of her car keys jingling as she would set off for, yet another day filled with purpose and determination. Her life was a whirlwind of activity, yet she never seemed rushed. She balanced her professional ambitions with familial duties, embodying a rare blend of efficiency and empathy.

Her words have remained with me over the years: "If you're willing to work, listen, and take mental notes, there's no dream too big to pursue." These weren't just motivational quotes but principles she lived by. Her life was a testament to her advice. Aunt Helen taught me that success isn't just about achieving personal milestones; it's about nurturing the dreams of others and creating opportunities where none seemed to exist.

Aunt Helen was more than a supporter of our family; she was the architect of our American dream. She meticulously orchestrated our journey to a new land brimming with opportunities and promises. I remember the countless conversations we had about the challenges and triumphs of our immigrant experience. Her strategic mind and compassionate heart guided us through the difficulties of adjusting to a new country, turning potential hardships into steppingstones for our success.

Without Aunt Helen's unwavering support and guidance, our path to America might have remained a distant, unreachable dream. Her influence extended beyond the tangible achievements she helped us realize; she imbued our family with a sense of purpose and direction. Her faith in us was a driving force that propelled us forward, turning obstacles into opportunities.

But Aunt Helen's impact went far beyond material success. She imparted a profound lesson that has shaped my perspective on life: true greatness lies not solely in personal achievements but in the ability to uplift and empower those around us. Her legacy is not merely one of financial prosperity; it is a testament to the power of kindness, generosity, and a steadfast belief in the potential of others. Aunt Helen's life was a masterclass in empathy and leadership, and her influence continues to ripple through our lives, guiding us to be better individuals and contributing to a world that reflects the values she held dear.

Her legacy lives on in the countless lives she touched, in the dreams she helped nurture, and in the indelible mark she left on all who were fortunate enough to know her. As we navigate our own paths, her example remains a constant reminder that true success is measured by the positive impact we have on others and the enduring legacy of love and support we leave behind.

DAD, EMILIO (AKA EMIL)

My Parents

Soon after graduating from high school, I decided to visit Israel. A deep longing to reunite with my biological father, a figure hidden in memories from my past, filled me with a mix of excitement and nervousness. When we finally met, his initial uncertainty gave way to a tender embrace, creating a rush of emotions that brought us both into a space of profound connection and shared history.

One of the most cherished memories from that week riding on a camel in the dessert and our visit to the Dead Sea —a place that held special significance for me. Floating effort-lessly in its salty water, I found comfort in the warmth of the therapeutic waters and the knowledge that I was sharing this moment with my father, a man whose presence had been absent for much of my life.

Reuniting with my younger siblings was both heart-warming and overwhelming. As I navigated the realization of being the oldest of sixteen, I was met with an outpouring of love and acceptance that surrounded me like a comforting blanket. My brothers Shimon, Amos, and I grew extremely close, our bonds deepening over time. Shimon became the voice of our family, whose wisdom and guidance I cherished. Amos, now a successful entrepreneur living in China, has become someone I admired and respected.

Despite the geographical distance that separated us, my father remained a pillar of strength and wisdom in our lives. His role as head lifeguard in Haifa spoke to his dedication to serving others, and his passing was mourned by thousands who had been touched by his kindness and bravery.

Looking back at my father's life and legacy, I've come to understand the importance of cherishing the moments we have with loved ones and the impact that even the simplest acts of kindness can have on those around us. His unwavering love and commitment to his family and community serve as an example—a reminder that our actions, no matter how small, can leave a positive mark on the lives of others. As we continue to honor his memory, we strive to emulate the values he held dear—kindness, compassion, and the belief that each of us has the power to make a difference in the lives of those around us.

In the end, my father's life taught me that true greatness lies not in grand gestures or accolades, but in the simple acts of love and kindness that we extend to one another each day. As I carry his memory in my heart, I am reminded of the profound effect that a life lived with purpose can have on the world around us.

PATERNAL GRANDPARENTS, ELIAHU AND LILA

In the heart of Livorno, Italy, a small but significant story unfolds—a tale of love, loss, and unwavering resilience, embodied by my grandmother, Lila. Born into a world that remains somewhat mysterious, her early life was marked by the quiet strength that would define her journey.

In the sun-drenched streets of Livorno, fate took a poignant turn when Lila crossed paths with my grandfather, a young medical student from Salonica, Greece. Their love blossomed against the backdrop of academia and vibrant life, leading to a marriage and the birth of their three beloved children—my aunts Emma and Rachel, and my father, Emilio. However, their happiness was brutally interrupted when World War II over took Europe. My grandfather, a Jewish doctor, fell victim to the horrific violence of the war. In a deeply tragic attack, he was beaten and publicly humiliated in the town square of Salonica—as a symbol of the regime's and power, before being shot in the head. All while my grandmother and their young children watched behind a large tree unbeknownst to the brutal savages that took his life, an ordeal that left an indelible scar on our family's history.

Widowed and heartbroken, Lila was thrust into a world of unimaginable adversity. Her spirit, however, remained resilient and unbroken despite the profound loss. Through the darkness of war and personal tragedy, she stood with a courage that would become a cornerstone of her legacy. Her strength in the face of such profound grief has reverberated through the generations, a testament to her unyielding fortitude and enduring love.

Lila

In the face of such loss, Lila arose as a beacon of courage, collaborating with the resistance to defy tyranny and create hope in a world turned upside down. With quiet determination, she risked her life to pass vital information to the Allies, making her a silent hero in the shadows of war. Each year, her bravery and sacrifice are honored, a testament to the strength of her character.

Amid the chaos of conflict, Lila's love for her children remained constant. As the war neared its end, she orchestrated their escape from Greece to the safety of Livorno, Italy, ensuring their survival amidst war-torn Europe.

But Lila's journey didn't end there. After the war, she found comfort in the arms of a new love and embarked on a new chapter of her life in Tunisia. Together, they built a path of perseverance and hope, laying the groundwork for a brighter future.

In 1949, as winds of change swept through the world, Lila and her family set sail for Israel—a land of dreams and possibilities. It was here, in her new homeland, that Lila's legacy truly took root—a legacy of love, compassion, and strength.

At the age of 105, Lila departed this world, leaving behind a legacy that transcends time. In the hearts of her family and community, she remains a symbol of strength, her laughter echoing in my memories, and her spirit ever-present beside me.

Lila's story teaches us that even in the darkest of times, love can triumph over hardship. Her life is a testament to the resilience of the human spirit, a shining example of courage in the face of adversity. As we honor her memory, we are reminded of the invaluable lesson she imparted—that in the end, it is love that binds us together, guiding us through the darkest nights and into the light of a new day.

In their memory, my granddaughter Lila-Star is named after Lila, and Germaine-Star, and my grandson Elijah is named after Eliahu.

CHAPTER FOUR

THE LAND OF MILK AND HONEY

> *"Growing up in Israel, the fiery furnace of childhood molds us with resilience, hope, and the courage to face each new dawn with unwavering spirit."*
>
> — *JEANETTE WINTERSON*

MY BIRTHPLACE, HAIFA, ISRAEL

In the heart of a land soaked in ancient history, ongoing conflict, and rich culture, I was born on August 15, 1952, in Haifa, Israel. My birth came just four years after the establishment of the state of Israel—a momentous time for our people. Our nation's history had been profoundly shaped by the three decades of British Mandate rule, from 1918 to 1948, which left an permanent mark on the landscape, politics, and destiny of our people. This was a time of both great hope and significant challenge, as we embarked on the journey of building a new nation from the ashes of the past.

Growing up in this young nation, my childhood was marked by the stark realities of life in a place where safety was a luxury and uncertainty a constant companion. The proximity of Lebanon to our neighborhood meant that sirens and alarms were a regular part of our lives, driving us into bunkered bomb shelters during frequent retaliations. The constant threat of conflict was a reality we all had to live with, shaping our daily routines and implanting in us a resilience that became second nature.

Despite the challenges, Israel was a land filled with tenacity and determination. In the aftermath of the Holocaust, our nation welcomed Jewish immigrants from every corner of the globe, creating communities rich in diverse cultures and traditions. This influx of people spurred rapid growth, leading to an urgent need for expansion in housing, infrastructure, and support for burgeoning farming communities.

Through these pivotal years, Israel grew into a prosperous nation. From humble beginnings in 1948, when the population was just 805,900—649,000 of whom were Jews—our nation has grown into a thriving economic powerhouse with a current population of over 9 million. Throughout history, Israel has often been described as the land of milk and honey, a place of abundance and promise. Yet, our journey has been filled with trials and tribulations, as empires—Romans, Ottomans, and finally, the British—left their mark on our sacred soil.

Today, as I contemplate my homeland's tumultuous past and the present and its promising future, I am filled with pride and gratitude. Our nation stands as a testament to the resilience of the Israeli spirit—a commitment to creating a brighter tomorrow while honoring our past. We strive to be a place that welcomes all, regardless of gender, race, or religion, in the pursuit of peace and unity among cultures.

As a young child, I watched my mother's heart break and piece itself back together countless times. When I was just two years old, my mother remarried, bringing a man into our lives who seemed to be the answer to her prayers—a charismatic Italian immigrant with striking blue eyes and an irresistible charm. But behind his charm lay a darker truth: he was irresponsible, addicted to gambling, and unable to provide the stability our family needed.

Growing up with my stepfather was an emotional rollercoaster. At first, he brought a sense of adventure into our lives, but over time, his long absences and financial irresponsibility left us struggling to make ends meet. My mother worked tirelessly, taking on double shifts at the hospital to support us, while my stepfather drifted in and out of our lives, leaving chaos in his wake.

I quickly became a stand-in mother to my siblings, shouldering the responsibility of caring for them while my mother worked long hours, often taking double shifts. My mornings were a rush to get everyone ready for school and walk them there, while evenings were filled with cooking and cleaning. Even though I was just a child myself, I had no choice but to grow up fast and assume the role of caregiver. We were latchkey kids, navigating the challenges of our daily lives with a maturity far beyond our years.

Despite the challenges, I found solace in my studies. Education became my refuge—a place where I could excel and challenge myself. School became my sanctuary, where I could focus solely on myself—my actions, my work, and my dreams. Winning my first prize for memorizing Latin plant names brought a rare moment of joy in an otherwise bleak world. I consistently earned high marks and excelled in all my subjects. During parent-teacher conferences, my achievements were always praised, but eventually, my mother stopped attending these meetings, choosing instead to focus on my siblings.

But there were also moments of heartache and unpleasantness. Weekly, I had to pluck feathers from freshly slaughtered chickens—a task I dreaded, but one that was necessary to ensure my family had food to eat. Each time I saw other children playing and laughing, I felt a pang of envy for the carefree childhood I longed for but could not have.

Through it all, my mother remained the backbone of our family. Her sacrifices and unwavering love nurtured the enduring spirit that I carry within me today. As I reflect on those difficult years, I am filled with a mixture of sadness for the childhood I never had and gratitude for the lessons in resilience, determination, and love that shaped me.

OUR MODULAR HOME, ACCO, ISRAEL

We finally found a place to call our own: a cramped, two hundred square feet duplex family modular home on a small plot of land. The house was poorly constructed, with inadequate insulation that left us shivering in winter and sweltering in summer. The interior consisted

Our Modular Home

of four small rooms, a kitchen, and an outdoor bathroom and shower stall. We showered on Fridays and took sponge baths in the middle of the week.

I washed our family's clothes and hung them on a makeshift clothesline. Our home was perhaps the most neglected in the neighborhood, with overgrown cacti and tall weeds making it difficult to walk through the yard. Life blended the bitter and the sweet, a constant battle between despair and hope.

Springtime held a special place in my heart. Our yard bloomed with wild daisies and vibrant red poppies, offering a sanctuary from our daily struggles. Lifting our spirit we played hide and seek among the towering wildflowers, crafting wreaths and garlands while pretending to be royalty from distant lands. As summer faded and the weeds dried up, we eagerly anticipated the return of spring, longing for its renewal.

At school, multi-colored tights were all the rage, but I lacked the means to join in. My mother wore black tights to work, patched with countless mends for warmth. Desperate to fit in, I asked if I could borrow them, and to my joy, she agreed. Rolling them up to my waist, I wore them proudly to school, savoring the sense of belonging they brought me. That day, the small gesture of acceptance meant the world to me, and the smile on my face couldn't be diminished. Even now, that feeling of fitting in stays with me. Today, I still strive for that same sense of belonging, though it often comes from within myself. Some days are more challenging than others, but just like my younger self, I continue to seek that acceptance. Now, it comes from what I feel confident in and what I find beautiful.

During this time, I co-founded a small social club at school with five friends. We met once a week to discuss a range of topics, from current events to our future aspirations to lift our spirit up. School was my sanctuary, a place where I found joy in learning. While math posed a considerable challenge, I endured with the help of a neighbor who tutored me, leading to significant improvement. I found solace in history the arts reading, writing, and even exploring my passion for cooking— a cherished pastime that still allows me to create unique dishes for loved ones.

Participating in extracurricular activities, like performing in the lead role of a school play, filled me with pride and a sense of accomplishment. I had devoted significant effort to practice and prepare for the role. However, when I learned that we couldn't afford to purchase a clay water jug required for the performance, I faced a tough decision. To ensure the production could proceed smoothly, I requested to be moved to a more minor role in the play.

English class was a highlight of my school days, especially when we received our first reading and writing book. To personalize mine, I covered it with a shopping bag and drew scenes from our neighborhood. This book became a cherished possession. I've always loved hearing stories, and I especially cherished listening to my South African friend Michal and her family converse in English. Their conversations, filled with rich accents and unique expressions, fascinated me. Even now, I delight in sharing vivid stories about my own life with my grandchildren. There's something profoundly rewarding about connecting with others through storytelling, passing on experiences and memories that create lasting bonds.

Amidst the bustling activity in the neighborhood, I sought ways to earn extra cash. I joined the hunt for scraps of steel and copper to sell by weight to a local vendor. One day, I explored an abandoned two-story Arabic house, thrilled by the prospect of finding valuable materials. As I navigated its corridors and staircases, my excitement soared when I discovered a long steel post embedded in a cement block. Despite my best efforts to extract it using fireclay, I was unsuccessful and left with only a handful of rusty nails. However, those nails proved surprisingly valuable. I repurposed them, along with unraveled old sweaters, into long scarves through self-taught knitting. Reflecting on these experiences' years later, I recognize the unpredictability of life and the importance of making thoughtful decisions when opportunities arise, whether they seem favorable or challenging.

THE PEOPLE OF MY CHILDHOOD

Mom's friend Rita, originally from India, was married to a Tunisian man who worked alongside my mom at the hospital. Together, they had three children. Rita was vibrant and full of life. I found joy in listening to their conversations in English and Hindi, though I longed to fully understand their words.

When I first visited Israel, I invited Rita to lunch, reminiscing about the fun times we had shared. However, I noticed a stark change in her demeanor; once lively and spirited, she now seemed reserved and had gained a considerable amount of weight. It saddened me to see this transformation, as if the vitality had been drained from her, especially since her children had moved away to start their own families.

Daisy, a close friend born in Tunisia, was fluent in French, Hebrew, and Arabic, much like my mother. Her husband, George, a botanist born in Germany, was equally multilingual. Despite their contrasting physical appearances—Daisy was pleasantly plump, while George was tall and robust—they shared a remarkable bond. Their greenhouse, filled with an array of plants, became our classroom where we learned their botanical names. Their love story, forged in Tunisia, was one of resilience and hope, as George had lost his first family during the Holocaust and found solace in building a new life with Daisy. Our weekly visits to their home were a highlight, filled with warmth, affection, and delicious food.

THE PARK...

Like many children in our neighborhood, Saturdays were a cherished break from the regular routines of school and work, as schools closed in observance of the Sabbath. This weekly break offered a rare opportunity for us to escape the demands of our structured lives. On those Saturdays, the park became our asylum. It was a place where the boundaries of daily life seemed to dissolve, allowing us to indulge in carefree play.

The park was more than just a playground; it was a canvas for our imaginations. We ran freely, our laughter echoing through the air as we played games, invented stories, and explored every nook and cranny. The grass beneath our feet felt soft and comforting, and the scent of blooming flowers mingled with the sounds of joyful chatter.

For me, these Saturdays were a precious gift. They provided a rare chance to shed the weight of responsibility that accompanied my daily life. It was on these days that I felt truly liberated, able to embrace the freedom to be myself without the constraints of my usual roles and duties. In the park, I could forget the challenges and simply revel in the joy of being a child.

These moments of unfiltered joy and freedom became the highlights of my week, a welcome contrast to the more serious aspects of life. They served as a reminder of the simple pleasures that could be found amidst the routine, and they left a lasting impression on me, shaping my appreciation for the small but meaningful escapes that life offers.

Reflecting on my childhood in Israel, I am reminded of a time characterized by perseverance and growth. From our humble beginnings in a cramped modular home to navigating financial hardships and seeking acceptance at school, each challenge left an indelible mark on my journey. Yet, amid these trials, there was a persistent sense of resilience—a fierce determination to press on against the odds.

In the face of adversity, the warmth of friendships and the unwavering support of our community provided a beacon of hope. These experiences taught me the profound lesson of finding joy even in difficult times and underscored the value of perseverance. They molded my character, instilling in me a deep appreciation for life's simple pleasures and a steadfast belief in the strength of the human spirit.

As I look back, I am profoundly grateful for the resilience that carried me through those formative years. It has guided me with strength and love into the future, preparing me to face the challenges that were coming my way.

CHAPTER FIVE

BREAKING THE SILENCE

 "There is no greater agony than bearing an untold story inside you."

— *MAYA ANGELOU*

I want to begin this chapter with a trigger warning, as it discusses sexual abuse. Writing this chapter has been the most challenging task I've faced so far. It forces me to relive an experience I'd much rather leave buried. However, I find myself here, writing in the hope of finding closure for my past trauma. As I write and release these words, I aim for them to be a source of strength for anyone who has faced or is still facing the trauma and terrors inflicted upon them.

My journey with this experience began when I was merely six years old and lasted for several years. The silence I maintained about the abuse has haunted me for over six decades. The long-reaching effects seeped into various areas of my life, robbing me of the sense of security every young child needs due to the mental and emotional abuse I suffered. Unfortunately, I could never verbalize these thoughts and feelings because I was consumed by the fear of what speaking out would mean and the realization that no one seemed to think it was wrong.

Even today, the shards of that abuse remain at the forefront of my mind. Though I have grown and processed my trauma, some nights, as soon as I close my eyes, it resurfaces, forcing me to relive vivid and powerful memories that are impossible to forget.

THE SPICE SHED

In front of my grandmother's house stood a quaint shed, its weathered door slightly ajar, revealing a collection of exquisite spice jars neatly arranged on a high shelf. The air was filled with the rich scents of cumin, coriander, paprika, and turmeric, each spice telling a story of distant lands and treasured memories. The shed was more than just a storage space; it was a symbol of my grandmother's love, a place where the aromas created a comforting embrace every time we stepped near. Despite its modest exterior, the shed held a world of wonders within its walls, a sanctuary that beckoned us with promises of adventure and laughter. My siblings and I often sought refuge there during our spirited games of hide and seek, finding joy amidst the shelves brimming with spices. Little did we know darker shadows lurked within those comforting walls, waiting to overshadow the positive memories we held dear.

One late afternoon, as the sun cast long shadows across the horizon, I found myself drawn to the familiar call of a trusted family member. His voice led me toward the shed, its ancient door creaking on its hinges as we stepped inside. The door closed behind us with a resounding click, a sound that would mark the beginning of a nightmare.

Initially, the atmosphere seemed harmless, just as it always did when filled with laughter and playful interactions. But the familiar laughter soon dissolved into something far more sinister. His touch was no longer innocent, and with a sudden, terrifying shift, I found myself on a rough-hewn cot, the impact jolting me into a chilling awareness of what was happening. Fear gripped me as I realized this was no innocent game.

Confusion clouded my thoughts as I struggled to comprehend the sudden change. The shed, once a safe haven of childhood secrets and adventures, now felt like a prison, its walls closing in around me. I silently pleaded for release, desperate to escape the nightmare that had unfolded. Yet, amidst the chaos of emotions, one question remained: Why?

In the innocence of youth, I was crushed beneath the weight of an experience I couldn't fully understand. As my small-framed body yielded to my abuser, I closed my eyes, seeking refuge in the darkness that surrounded me. In that silent space, tears refused to fall, but anger and fear raged within me. I was thrust into a place where time stood still, and the anguish seemed endless.

For six decades, I existed in a state of numbed agony, keeping my abuse a secret. My spirit was tethered to an injured body like a fragile bird, unable to fly. I couldn't comprehend the depths of my torment, remaining trapped within the confines of my silence. The shed, once a refuge, became a place of horror, its walls bearing witness to an unspeakable act perpetrated by someone who should have been a protector.

When I finally found the courage to break my silence at the age of eighteen and confide in my mother, her response was not the comforting embrace I had hoped for. Instead, it was a deafening silence, followed by the familiar tone of victim-blaming: "Why didn't you say something sooner?" Those words hung heavy in the air, crushing whatever hope I had left. In that moment of betrayal, I realized that my journey toward healing would be a solitary one, filled with obstacles and uncertainties, as my mother couldn't confront the demons of my past. Yet, despite the hardship, a flame of resilience grew within me, protecting the most vulnerable parts of myself.

For years, I built barriers around my heart, shielding it from further harm. I became a fortress, fiercely protecting my daughters from the world. It was only through therapy that I began to unravel the complexities of my trauma and find the courage to reclaim my voice. Every word I spoke was a victory, hard-won through the long process of self-discovery and healing. Even as I found comfort in my family loves embrace, doubt lingered, creating challenges in my relationships. However, the scars of my past tested my husband's unwavering devotion, and through our struggles, we forged a deep bond built on resilience, love, and respect. He stood by me when it seemed like no one else would.

When my past traumas resurface, anger simmers just beneath the surface, fueled by the failures of a legal system that often does not deliver justice to those who have suffered unspeakable horrors.

The lack of universal statutes of limitations on sexual abuse only perpetuates the cycle of victimization, allowing perpetrators to evade accountability. But while abusers may try to discredit our memories, the truth remains. It is imperative that we continue to raise our voices, demanding justice for ourselves and those whose cries have been silenced by the passage of time. Without accountability, the cycle of abuse continues, serving as a harsh reminder of the consequences of inaction. I've become a vocal advocate for harsher sentencing laws regarding child abuse and remain committed to standing against sexual predators, this abuse is practiced and in some cultures it's considered very common, I say this practice is an outrage to all the that have experienced it . In sharing my story, I have deliberately chosen not to name the perpetrators, for they are undeserving of recognition.

In reaching out to others who walk a similar path, I

discovered a sense of purpose that transcended my pain and the power of forgiveness. How I choose to live, how my daughters choose to live and how my grandchildren choose to live, that we actually have a chance to break generational traumas and patterns. Through shared stories and struggles, I found comfort in knowing I was not alone. I learned to embrace my scars as proof of the strength within me, a reminder that I am more than the sum of my trauma. Though the road ahead is challenging, I walk it with renewed purpose, believing that together we can create a world where survivors are heard and celebrated for their courage and strength.

CHAPTER SIX

SMALL LUXURIES

 "Enjoy the little things, for one day you may look back and realize they were the big things."

— *ROBERT BRAULT*

TELEVISION BROADCASTS FROM JORDAN (1956)

In 1956, television broadcasts from Jordan brought a wave of excitement to our neighborhood. Though televisions were expensive, a few lucky neighbors managed to purchase them. They generously allowed us kids to gather outside their living room windows, eager to catch a glimpse of this new form of entertainment. We climbed onto windowsills, clinging tightly as we vied for the best view. We eagerly awaited the tiny white dots and sounds transmitted from Jordan and Egypt. Even though many of us didn't understand Arabic, we were mesmerized by the blurry images on the small screen.

This pastime didn't last long, but it reminds me of how we cherished the simple pleasures in life. Today, you can buy and install a smart television in every room of your house within minutes. Eventually, our neighbors grew tired of the crowded group of kids invading their privacy, laughing and talking loudly. To deter us, they dumped buckets of cold water outside their window, creating a huge, muddy puddle. And just like that, our television-watching adventures came to an end.

The only luxury my mother purchased was a small refrigerator. We were thrilled to enjoy ice cubes, marking the end of the old ice boxes and the arrival of new, innovative appliances. However, life wasn't without its challenges. A tornado struck our neighborhood in Israel, destroying half the homes and causing significant damage to many roofs, including ours. The strong winds blew away half of our roof, leaving a trail of destruction. In that uncertain world, we feared what might come next. The scariest part was hearing some adults predict the end of the world because of the tornado. Their fears were contagious, and it was terrifying to think about what could happen.

THE TWO SIDES OF MY STEPFATHER, VICTOR

Feral cat were rampant in our neighborhood. My stepfather and a couple of his friends found an enjoyment tormenting them. They attached meat to a fishing lure and waited for the cats to bite. When the cats got close, they were caught, flying into the air and letting out horrible shrieks before being released. It was sadistic and seeing that side of my stepfather disturbed me. He also enjoyed target shooting, considering himself a marksman. My job was to pluck the feathers from the dead pigeons on the ground floor.

Despite this, he wasn't unkind to us. We loved him. He was always happy, seemingly unaffected by anything. At least, I never saw him distressed. He seemed unfazed by my mother's yelling frustrations and anger. He rarely raised his voice or scolded us. He wasn't overly affectionate, he considered me as his own daughter, and everyone loved him for his fun and engaging nature. However, little did they know about his personal life, nor did they care enough to ask.

Once we moved to the United States, I don't remember our family ever being invited to his friends' or acquaintances. Though our apartment was always welcoming to everyone, and he was a great cook. When he returned home after a long absence, the money was used for cooking and entertaining everyone.

Reflecting on those times, I've learned valuable lessons about resilience and compassion. Despite the hardships and the troubling actions of those around me, I found solace in the small joys and the love of my family. The refrigerator, a simple luxury, brought us immense joy and symbolized progress and hope for a better future. The community gatherings and holiday celebrations showed me the importance of together-ness and the power of traditions to uplift our spirits, even in the face of adversity.

The cruelty I witnessed, particularly from my stepfather, taught me about the importance of kindness and empathy. His actions were a stark reminder that cruelty, whether towards animals or people, is never justifiable. This understanding has influenced my approach to life, making me more compas-sionate and determined to treat all living beings with respect.

Ultimately, these experiences have shaped my values and outlook on life. I've learned that while we cannot always control our circumstances or the actions of others, we can choose to respond with kindness, find joy in the small things, and remain resilient in the face of adversity. It's essential to cherish the good moments and learn from the difficult ones, as they all contribute to our growth and character.

Looking back, I am grateful for the lessons learned and the strength gained from those early experiences. They have taught me to appreciate small luxuries, to value family and community, and to stand firmly against cruelty. These princi-ples guide me today as I strive to create a life filled with kindness, joy, and resilience, regardless of the challenges that come my way.

THE COUCH

In the bustling streets of our neighborhood, a weekly tradition played out as an Arab vendor atop his camel made his rounds, announcing his ripe watermelons and cantaloupes. The aroma of fresh fruit mingled with the lively chatter of children, drawing us in like bees to a flower. As the camel knelt down, its large form casting a shadow over the cobblestones, we gathered around in wide-eyed wonder, our laughter filling the air with the simple joy of childhood.

My childhood in Israel was filled with moments like these —simple, joyful, and full of wonder. I still remember the day my mother returned home from work with a single pear, cradled in her hand like a precious treasure. Fruit was a rare treat, and as she sliced the pear, its sweet juices dripping down our chins, I savored a moment of pure bliss that stayed with me long after.

Years later, when I returned to Israel in 1970, the landscape had changed. The quaint streets of my childhood had been replaced by towering high-rise buildings, and familiar landmarks were overshadowed by the city's growth. Yet, despite these changes, fragments of my past remained—a small park where we once played, now dwarfed by the surrounding structures. The echoes of my childhood still lingered, reminding me of the simple pleasures that once filled those streets.

As I walked through the familiar streets of my old neighborhood, memories surfaced with each step. A chance encounter with our former neighbors brought those memories into sharper focus, their warm greetings pulling me back to those earlier days. Amidst the lighthearted banter, one invitation stood out—an offer to sit and talk, which would unravel emotions I hadn't expected to revisit.

Seated on a weathered porch beneath a makeshift canopy, I found myself on an old, tattered couch—a relic from the past. As I settled into its worn cushions, a wave of nostalgia washed over me. The couch seemed to hold the essence of my mother's presence, a silent reminder of the life we shared.

In a moment of reflection, I asked about the origins of the couch, feeling a need to connect with my past. The response confirmed a truth I had long suspected. The realization hit me hard, and tears welled up as memories long buried resurfaced. I reached out to touch the worn fabric of the couch, each thread a testament to the countless moments it had witnessed. It felt like a bridge to a time when life was simpler, and our family was whole.

As I sat there, the weight of my realization grew heavier, filling the air with a mix of longing and gratitude. I couldn't help but think of my mother, who had transformed our humble home into a place of warmth and comfort through tireless effort and sacrifice. Her presence seemed to linger in every corner, a reminder of the strength and love she had poured into our lives.

With these thoughts in mind, I returned to Los Angeles, carrying with me the echoes of my mother's unspoken dreams. The urge to confront my stepfather about the past was strong, but I chose to preserve the fragile peace my mother had worked so hard to maintain. Some truths, I realized, were best left in the past.

CHAPTER SEVEN

LEAVING ISRAEL

 "Loneliness and the feeling of being unwanted is the most terrible poverty."

— *MOTHER TERESA*

1964 ISRAEL

I remember the day we left Israel so vividly. It was both exciting and nerve-wracking—the uncertainty of the future weighed heavily on my mind. Saying goodbye to my classmates and neighbors, on my last day at school was a somber affair, the significance of the moment hanging in the air. We hurriedly packed a few of our clothes into old, tattered suitcases. My stepdad seemed unfazed by the impact and was delighted to return to his homeland, offering no explanation, which left me feeling bewildered and anxious.

He purchased four one-way tickets on a Greek cargo ship sailing from Haifa, Israel, to Naples, Italy. As the ship loaded and unloaded cargo at various other ports of call, I realized that his plan was not to return to Israel. Knowing that my mom would return home, my stepdad asked me to get ready a few days before we left. "Just our clothes," he said. "We'll buy the rest in Italy." I began packing my personal items—one of my most cherished possessions, a satin yellow handkerchief holder that I hand-stitched when I was seven years old, along with a few treasured books and a handful of clothes. Each item I packed felt like a piece of my heart, my childhood slipping away with every fold of fabric. I was confused and saddened to leave behind our life, our school friends, teachers, and neighbors.

I can still recall the smell of the sea air, the warmth of the sun, and the creaking sound of the boat's floor beneath my worn-out shoes as we boarded. We settled into the lower deck, where we slept among the hired crew. The constant rocking of the boat causing my siblings and me to constantly throw up. The voyage seemed endless. We weren't allowed to disembark at any port, remaining on the boat for the entire journey to Naples. The living conditions were harsh—hot and musty, with the red-stained floors showing wear and tear, peeling beneath our feet. It was clear this was no luxury ship. I was expected to help the cook in the kitchen, and as I worked, I watched the beautiful landscape of Israel disappear from view, wishing I could jump into the blue, warm ocean and swim back home.

Throwing up became a daily occurrence. The voyage, with stops in Athens, Cyprus, and numerous other islands to load and unload cargo, lasted fifteen days. It felt like an eternity. When we finally disembarked in Naples, Italy, we were greeted by the chaotic sight of sidewalks filled with mountains of garbage. The pungent stench made my stomach churn. I later learned that this was a result of the infamous garbage strikes that would continue to plague Italy for decades. We finally boarded a train to Genoa, Italy, a 367-mile, eight-hour journey to be reunited with our mother and baby brother.

The train ride felt endless, the rhythmic clatter of wheels on tracks a constant reminder of how far we were from home.

I stared out the window, watching the Italian countryside blur past, feeling a mix of awe and sadness. The vibrant greens and rolling hills contrasted sharply with the turmoil in my heart. I clung to my satin yellow handkerchief holder, a tangible piece of my past in this uncertain future.

When we arrived in Genoa, we were greeted by our aunt in her small, crowded living room. She was a tall woman, resembling my stepdad—larger than life, flamboyant, and direct. I had met her years before when she visited Israel, but it felt different this time. Her two young children, who were the same age as us, stood nearby, speaking in Italian we didn't understand. They were kind and friendly, but somewhat confused by our arrival. Our aunt seemed bewildered and overwhelmed by our presence, watching quietly as my parents interacted.

We were dirty, tired, and hungry from the long journey; we stretched our arms and embraced our mom ever so tenderly. She stood stone-faced, her eyes fixed on my stepdad's blank gaze. Without a moment's hesitation, she moved quickly across the room and slapped him so hard it echoed through the cramped space. He stood there, emotionless and speechless, fully aware of his careless, irresponsible actions. She said, "What did you do? I will never return to Israel, to our home. How could you do this to our family? This is a nightmare. How could you?" She started to cry. I felt so saddened and understood her pain. I walked slowly to her, gently embraced her, and whispered words of comfort in Hebrew, promising that everything would be okay and that one day we would return home. Twenty years later, I fulfilled that promise, taking my mom back to Israel, where she finally found the closure she so desperately needed.

Those words still echo in my mind. From that moment, the trajectory of our lives shifted irreversibly. My stepdad, notorious for his gambling, had wagered our home, our land, and all the new furnishings my mom had bought just two weeks before leaving Israel with my baby brother. I held him responsible for our situation from that point forward. We left behind everything we had known—our country, our life, our friends, and all we held dear. The feeling of security vanished into thin air.

Our new life in Italy was a sharp contrast to what we had known. The sights and sounds were foreign and fascinating, but they couldn't fill the void left by the sudden upheaval. The crowded apartment became a small world of its own, filled with the scents of Italian cooking and the constant hum of unfamiliar words. My aunt's kitchen, though cramped, was a haven of rich aromas—garlic sautéing in olive oil, fresh basil, simmering tomato sauce, and pasta. I found solace in these small pleasures, clinging to them amidst the chaos of our uprooted lives.

Despite the tension and uncertainty, there were moments of beauty. I remember the bright, sunlit mornings when we would venture out into the narrow streets of the neighborhood food markets. The cobblestone paths led us past ancient buildings adorned with vibrant flowers spilling over balconies. The laughter of children playing echoed through the alleys, a universal sound that needed no translation.

Yet, every night, the reality of our situation settled back in. The cramped quarters, the strained silences, and the ever-present worry about what would come next weighed heavily on us. My mom's resilience during this time was remarkable. She worked tirelessly to make the best of our circumstances, cooking meals from the limited supplies we had and ensuring that we felt some semblance of normalcy.

As time passed, we adapted to our new surroundings. My siblings and I learned bits and pieces of Italian, enough to communicate with our cousins and navigate the local market. We found a rhythm in our daily lives, balancing the remnants of our past with the uncertainties of our future.

One day, I overheard my mom and aunt talking in hushed

tones. My mom's voice, usually steady and strong, wavered with emotion. She spoke of her dreams for us, her fears, and her unwavering determination to create a better life despite the hardships. It was a moment that struck me deeply, a testament to her enduring spirit and love for us.

Within a week of our arrival, our aunt rented an apartment in the suburbs of Genoa, a thirty-minute drive from the city center. It was a newly built, three-story building with a two-bedroom apartment on the second floor. The apartment window faced a very busy street, and she generously paid for our first and last month's rent. A few days later, we moved in.

The neighborhood consisted of working middle-class families. We were astonished to find our apartment already furnished with the most beautiful ornate antique furnishings. Dark, carved woods and bird's eye maple armoires graced the rooms; the bedding featured freshly laundered, crisp white cotton sheets and warm blankets. The dining room chairs, carved lion heads on the armrests, were museum-quality treasures. The kitchen was fully stocked with the most exquisite etched crystal stemware and dishes that belonged to my stepdad's affluent family. These items, hidden away in storage during the war to protect them from the Nazis, were a silent reminder of a more prosperous past. Yet, despite the elegance, the apartment felt cold and impersonal.

Every day, the once-beautiful apartment became a symbol of sorrow, sadness, and loneliness, replacing the joy it should have brought. The walls that were supposed to reverberate with laughter instead felt cold and hollow. My stepdad's family, who might have been a source of comfort, remained distant and indifferent, their visits so rare that they felt more like formalities than genuine connections. It was as if we had been uprooted not just from our homeland but from any sense of belonging or support. Years later, I returned to Italy in search of the family ties I had longed for, reconnecting with cousins who had built families of their own. The reunion was bittersweet, filled with both warmth and a lingering sadness, as I sought the closure that had evaded me for so many years.

My mom was overwhelmed and sank into a deep depression. She had lost hope of ever returning to Israel, and our future seemed very bleak. Without money or prospects, and with no means of financial support, we found ourselves very hungry within a few weeks. The clothes we brought from Israel were inadequate for the harsh winter, barely keeping us warm.

Learning a new language was a small spark of excitement amid the gloom. I found Italian to be beautiful and lyrical, and I eagerly absorbed every word. My siblings and I clung to each other for support and comfort. Our mother, understanding the gravity of our situation, knew that without hope, we wouldn't be able to survive in this foreign land. I dreamed of returning home to Israel, our Jewish state. Genoa, with its ancient history and beauty, felt alien and unwelcoming. The churches dominated every aspect of Italian daily life, a stark contrast to what we were used to.

Within days of our arrival, my stepdad's supposed new job prospects vanished, leaving us to fend for ourselves. He came in and out of our lives, all blurring into one long struggle. We found it increasingly hard to hold on to our memories of Israel; it was too painful. From time to time, our dad would reappear, bringing a few bags of food. He felt like a distant acquaintance rather than a father. He tried to make us laugh and calm us down, but it wasn't what we needed. His attempts were fruitless. We needed stability.

He continued to devise new schemes, one of which involved fabricating a story about winning the largest lottery in the city of Piacenza. He manipulated his sister into giving him an advance on his supposed winnings. My aunt loved her brother and dismissed the entire incident.

His gambling addiction continued to escalate, destroying every opportunity he had to provide for us and sabotaging our lives. My mom was left to carry the heavy burden of raising us alone in a country she neither embraced nor felt any allegiance to. Struggling each day to feed us.

Looking back on those years, I see that our struggles and hardships shaped who I am today. They taught me resilience, the importance of hope, and the value of family. My journey from the suburbs of Genoa to where I am now has been long and arduous, but it has also been filled with lessons that have guided me throughout my life. Through it all, I have learned that no matter how difficult life may seem, we must hold on to hope and cherish the moments of light amidst the darkness.

My primary focus, and often a heavy burden, was to help my siblings and my mom. There were times I felt utterly defeated, a quiet rebellion brewing inside me for years. I did my best to comfort my mom, who was deeply depressed. Our roles had reversed; I was now the adult, the anchor everyone relied on. Like my mom, I never saw our life in Italy as a permanent one. I felt drained and hopeless, frequently waking from terrible dreams and night sweats.

Not far from our apartment, we found solace in the beautiful countryside. The old stone houses, standing in a row for decades, and the abandoned plum orchards offered us juicy fruit to fill our empty stomachs. The picturesque landscape, with wildflowers glistening in the sunlight, reminded me of my backyard in Israel, where I used to wander aimlessly for hours. We felt the sun's warmth in the cold air, running and playing until dusk, only to return to our cold apartment at sunset.

We wandered daily, exploring the countryside and nearby hills without purpose or direction. It seemed odd to see people living in caves at the foot of the hills, yet they were the kindest, most cheerful, and most hospitable people. Despite our rusty Italian, they welcomed us with open arms, offering us their meager food, juice, hot coffee for my mom, and homemade cookies. Communicating was a struggle as they preferred the Genoa dialect, but we didn't care. We laughed and gestured with our hands, expressing our gratitude for their heartfelt hospitality. Back at the apartment, we quickly crawled under the covers to warm up and shut our eyes.

THE DAY WE FOUND JESUS

One vivid memory from our time in Italy was the day my sister and I, driven by hunger, decided to sneak over a neighbor's barbed wire fence. The rusty metal snagged at our clothes as we climbed, but the sight of the orchard on the other side, with its trees heavy with ripe, red apples, was too tempting to resist. The apples gleamed in the late afternoon sun, their bright red skin a stark contrast against the dark green leaves. We hurriedly picked as many as we could, our mouths watering at the thought of biting into the juicy fruit.

But our joy was short-lived. Suddenly, a man burst out of a nearby house, his face contorted in anger, yelling in Italian— a language we barely understood but knew enough to sense the threat in his voice. He waved a rake above his head as he charged towards us, his footsteps pounding the earth. Panic surged through us, and we bolted, dropping all but one of the apples in our frantic escape.

We ran blindly, our hearts racing, until we spotted a small, old building with its front door ajar. Without thinking, we darted inside, the cool darkness of the interior a stark contrast to the bright daylight we had just left behind. The room was large and dimly lit, the air thick with dust and the scent of old wood. Dark wooden chairs stood in perfect rows, their polished surfaces reflecting the faint light filtering through the stained-glass windows. The windows themselves were a riot of colors—reds, blues, and greens—casting a rainbow of light onto the opposite wall, creating an almost magical, yet eerie atmosphere.

In the center of the room stood a tall, open, rectangular wooden box, its height towering over us. We crouched behind it, our breathing shallow as we tried to calm our racing hearts. The stillness of the room was overwhelming, every creak of the floorboards under our feet echoing in the silence. The quiet was so profound that it felt as though time itself had stopped, leaving us suspended in a moment of pure, paralyzing fear. We dared not move, our imaginations running wild with what might happen next.

After what felt like an eternity, curiosity got the better of us. We slowly rose and peeked over the edge of the box, expecting to see something mundane, something that would break the tension. Instead, we were met with a sight that froze our blood. Inside the box lay a man, his hands folded neatly across his chest, his face serene yet lifeless. Blood seemed to ooze from his torso, staining his garments a deep, unnatural red. The horror of the sight gripped us, our minds struggling to comprehend what we were seeing.

Terrified, we turned and ran, the sound of our footsteps loud in the stillness as we fled the building, our fear propelling us as far from that place as our legs could carry us. We didn't stop until we were well out of sight, and even then, the image of the man haunted us. It wasn't until much later that we learned the truth—that the building was an old church, and the figure in the box was not a man at all, but a wooden carved statue of Jesus Christ. Yet, for us, the memory remained as vivid as ever, a chilling reminder of the day our childish adventure took a dark and unexpected turn.

CHAPTER EIGHT

SNAILS AND CINEMA

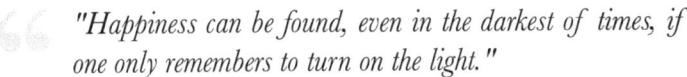

"Happiness can be found, even in the darkest of times, if one only remembers to turn on the light."

— *J.K. ROWLING*

THE DELICIOUS SNAILS

I n the third week of living in our new apartment, the sound of a loud television blaring and children giggling seeped through the walls from next door. To our surprise, our neighbor invited us to join her children in watching television. We were thrilled and eagerly awaited the afternoon, excited to spend time watching Italian cartoons. When the moment finally arrived, we found ourselves sitting on the hard, cold, marbled floor, laughing along with the funny cartoons. The joy, however, was short-lived, and we were devastated when the show ended. Unfortunately, that brief connection was fleeting, as our neighbor stopped inviting us over, leaving us longing for those simple, joyful moments that had quickly become a cherished memory.

One morning, after a light drizzle, I was exploring the

neighborhood near a vacant lot when I stumbled upon a cluster of squeamish, slimy snails inching their way through the wet grass. With childlike curiosity, I carefully folded my shirt, gathered the snails, and hurried back to our apartment with a paper bag in hand, I knocked on the neighbor's door, eager to show them to the children, I was greeted with a warm smile, the neighbor was so happy and took the bag to my surprise. She loved snails and planned to cook them for dinner.

That evening, we were once again invited to watch television, enjoying our favorite Mickey Mouse cartoons. Sitting on that same cold, marbled floor, with the flickering screen casting a warm glow on our faces, we felt a sense of belonging and comfort that transcended the language barrier. Each opportunity to gather around the television helped us escape and pass the time, creating moments of joy amidst the newness and uncertainty of our surroundings. These moments, though fleeting, were precious. They provided a sense of normalcy and happiness in an otherwise unfamiliar environment.

Many years later, while visiting our family in Paris, France, I was invited to a renowned Michelin-star restaurant. Ordering from the dinner menu, I chuckled when I saw escargot listed among the hors d'oeuvres. The memory of those snails and our Italian neighbor brought back a flood of nostalgia, and I couldn't help but feel a connection to that time and place.

SALESGIRL

Back then, my stepdad, ever the entrepreneur, came up with another quick money-making scheme: selling pantyhose packages, a hot item at the time. As his only and best salesgirl, I took on the challenge with enthusiasm. I walked up and down the stairs of nearby apartment buildings, knocking on doors and offering the packages for sale. My confidence shone through despite my limited Italian, relying heavily on hand gestures to communicate. By the end of each day, I had sold all the bundled packages. This venture lasted a couple of weeks until it abruptly ended when my stepdad stopped paying the supplier. During this time, I managed to sneak a few liras and secretly gave them to my mom, knowing it would help us in some small way.

The vivid memories of these experiences, from watching cartoons on a marbled floor to selling pantyhose in bustling apartment buildings, painted a colorful picture of my childhood. Each moment, filled with laughter, resourcefulness, and the warmth of human connection, remains etched in my mind, shaping who I am today. These experiences taught me resilience, creativity, and the importance of finding joy in the little things, no matter where life takes you.

THE THEATER

In our dreary world, light was something we had to seek out, and we found it in the dark of the cinema. My mother and I would purchase two tickets, always for the matinee. The afternoons felt less harsh, less heavy, in the glow of the silver screen. Then we would sneak my siblings who were, eager and hungry for adventure, in through the back door—our own little act of rebellion. It wasn't just about seeing the movie, though that part was magic; it was about escaping, even if just for a while.

The theater was always full, the air thick with the smell of buttery popcorn, our excitement palpable. I can still hear the sound of our laughter echoing, bouncing off the walls of that room, filling it up. It was the kind of laughter that made our bellies hurt—not from hunger this time, but from joy. We shared a single dessert, passing it carefully between us, each bite savored under the dim flicker of the screen. For those fleeting moments, the weight of our mother's sadness lifted, like dark clouds giving way to light.

In those afternoons, the cinema became our sanctuary, a place where the hardships of life slipped away, where our hearts could expand. We were like seeds of a pomegranate, clustered together in the dark, bound by something invisible yet strong. The film would wash over us, and for a few hours, we weren't struggling. We weren't hungry. We weren't afraid.

But the magic always had to end. The walk home was bittersweet, the streetlights casting a soft glow on the rain-slicked streets. We'd talk about the film, reenacting our favorite scenes, the laughter lingering even as reality crept back in. By the time we reached our small apartment, the weight of the world would return, pressing down on us once more. Yet, in the space between those moments, we had found something sacred—a reminder that even in darkness, there was light to be found. The seeds of joy, small and fleeting, but they were ours.

THE CEMETERY

On a beautiful late afternoon, my sister, brother, and I decided to visit the nearby Cimitero Monumentale di Staglieno, renowned for its monumental sculptures. As one of the largest cemeteries in Europe, built in 1851, it was the resting place of my stepdad's family and had always intrigued me. Growing up, I had heard stories about the ornate, marbled monuments and mausoleums that housed entire families. I was curious to explore their beauty and history.

We walked swiftly, eager to reach the Jewish burial site before sunset. The cemetery was vast, a labyrinth of intricately carved statues and solemn mausoleums. The late afternoon light cast long shadows, adding an air of mystery to the place. As we wandered through the silent rows of graves, the stillness was almost tangible. It felt as if we had stepped into another world, one where time stood still and memories lingered in the air.

Finally, we arrived at the Jewish burial site, but despite our efforts, we couldn't find the family graves we were looking for. The setting sun painted the sky in hues of orange and pink, and the cemetery grew eerier by the minute. The quiet was unsettling, and a sense of unease settled over us. I decided it was time to head back to our apartment.

We hurried toward the exit as the shadows deepened and the air grew cooler. I held my younger brother tightly, his small hand clasped in mine. Suddenly, I stumbled over a freshly dug grave, the earth soft and uneven beneath my feet. My imagination ran wild, and I felt as if a large hand might emerge from the grave and drag us down into the dark, deep hole.

We finally reached the massive wrought iron gate at the entrance just minutes before it closed. The tourist buses were gone, and the parking lot was empty, casting an eerie silence over the area. We ran as fast as we could, not daring to look back, our hearts pounding in our chests. The fifteen-minute walk back to our apartment felt like an eternity.

That experience left a lasting impression on me. To this day, I have never loved visiting cemeteries. The memory of that late afternoon at Staglieno, with its haunting beauty and silent, watchful statues, still sends shivers down my spine. The sense of unease and the vivid imagery of that place are etched in my mind, a reminder of the thin line between curiosity and fear.

CHAPTER NINE

A SAFE HAVEN

> *"Out of suffering have emerged the strongest souls; the*
> *most massive characters are seared with scars."*
>
> — *KHALIL GIBRAN*

CASA DELLA DONNA, A SHELTER FOR WOMEN
AND CHILDREN, TWO MONTHS, 1964

After two months living in Via Piacenza, our lives took the worst turn, we received an eviction notice. That day is etched in my memory: the sky was cold and cloudy, with a light drizzle adding to the gloom. We closed the door behind us, leaving our temporary home and all its contents. It reminded me of our rushed departure from Israel just months earlier. Carrying our suitcases and wrapped in the few blankets and clothes we had brought from Israel, we began to walk, taking comfort in each other's arms. My mom's face looked ashen and desperate, she was losing hope. I tried to cheer her up, but we were all exhausted, hungry, and lost, unsure of what to do next. I looked up at the sky, my heart heavy, and whispered, 'G-d, why is this happening again? Please, help us. Please...' My hand clenched into a fist, as if gripping onto hope, my eyes searching the heavens for an answer.

My stepdad was nowhere to be found. Unsure of where to turn, I pulled my two younger siblings close, doing my best to keep them calm while hiding my own fear. My mom held my baby brother, looking for shelter under a storefront awning. The sun set, we found ourselves homeless, unsure of where to turn for help. My mom cried softly tears began to flow with so much desperation, and we all felt that heavy weight descent upon us I tried to stay calm and strong, hoping that somehow we would find a way out of this mess.

As night fell and the streets grew eerily quiet, we huddled together, cold and unsure of what to do next. The days that followed were even harder—we had nowhere to go, no home, no place to find refuge. Then, like an angel, an elderly woman appeared, her eyes filled with warmth and tenderness. She exchanged a few soft words with my mother before handing her some money. As a bus pulled up, the woman spoke to the driver, ensuring we'd be safely taken to Casa Della Donna—the House of the Woman.

After a thirty-minute bus ride, we arrived at the shelter on the outskirts of town. The building was large and plain, but it was a place where we could find help. We were greeted by a kind elderly lady who led us to a room filled with rows of wooden tables and chairs. We sat quietly, surrounded by the sounds of crying babies and tired mothers trying to feed their children.

The women around us looked exhausted as they comforted their children and encouraged them to eat a simple meal of pasta with tomato sauce. We ate in silence, grateful for the warm food after days of going without. It was a small comfort in a very difficult time.

After dinner, we were shown to the bathrooms. The hot showers comforting it felt like a small relief, washing away our pain and sorrow. We were given donated pajamas and sweaters; we were ushered to a large room filled with single cots. Each cot had a blanket and a pillow, and we placed our belongings underneath, worried that someone might take them. Despite the challenges, we finally felt a bit of comfort as we slept through the night.

A loud bell woke us early the next morning. We quickly dressed and lined up for breakfast. After eating, we had to leave the shelter and wander the streets of Genoa until evening when we returning for dinner and sleep. This routine became our life existence for the next three months. It was a difficult time, and we often felt lonely unloved and worthless, praying for of a miracle to rescue us.

Having experienced homelessness, I now have a deep empathy for others in the same situation. We were incredibly poor, and it felt like no one cared if we lived or died. Each day brought new challenges, and the uncertainty of our future was overwhelming. But even in those dark times, I held on to hope for new beginnings.

When you see someone who is homeless, try to be kind and generous. Don't make assumptions about their situation. You never know what they have been through. Not all home-less people are on drugs or mentally ill—many are simply struggling through difficult circumstances.

VIA LUGO

With the help of the shelter's director, we eventually secured government-subsidized housing. Leaving the shelter behind, we were grateful for a place to call our own, even if it was just temporary.

Our new home in Via Lugo was in a housing project for

low-income families. It was a modest apartment on the fourth floor of a walk-up building, with two small bedrooms, a tiny kitchen, and a small bathroom. We used communal showers downstairs, which were available once a week for a small fee. The rest of the week, we relied on boiling water for sponge baths. We washed our clothes by hand and hung them out to dry on the small balcony. That balcony, with its view of the Mediterranean Sea, became my favorite spot. It gave me a sense of peace and a little hope for the future.

I have good memories of our time in that building. I often spent hours on the balcony, watching the massive cargo ships pass by. Their horns became a familiar and comforting sound in our daily lives.

Two floors below us, my mom became friends with a family from Calabria, an island in southern Italy. They were warm and kind, a welcome change from the hardships we had faced. They often invited us into their home, sharing delicious southern Italian meals and letting us watch television with them. They even helped by watching my younger siblings, which allowed my mom to find work as a caregiver for an elderly man.

Although our father was not consistently present, my mom remained strong, raising us as a single parent. She enrolled us in a Jewish school midway through the school year to ensure we received a good education and stayed connected to our heritage. Genoa's oldest and only synagogue played an important role in our lives, providing community services and a school for Jewish children. The teachers were excellent, and despite the challenge of learning a new language, we quickly adapted and immersed ourselves in Italian culture. Each day brought new challenges, but over time, it got easier, and we began to thrive in our new environment.

Every day, our driver Uzi picked us up for school and brought us home. He was a character, and we found his quirks amusing. The schools uniforms made us feel like we belonged, just like the other students. We especially looked forward to the hot lunches provided by the school. Beyond education, the school was a safe haven that connected us to the rich history of the Jewish community in Italy.

Italy started to feel like home, and one of the highlights was a school trip to Monaco on the French Riviera. I remember the beauty of the flower farms on the hillsides, the flowers sweet scent in the air, and the stunning view of the Mediterranean Sea. It was a day of joy and wonder, a memory I have revisited many times over the years.

As time went on, I excelled in my studies, mastering the Italian language and thriving academically. My teachers were engaging and made learning enjoyable. My time in Italy was a transformative period that shaped who I am today.

The Jewish holidays at school were special, continuing traditions that had been practiced for over 2,000 years. Hearing Hebrew spoken, even for part of the day, brought comfort and a connection to our heritage.

I developed a passion for learning and experiencing new things fueled by our daily route to school, which took us past Christopher Columbus's 500-year-old home, now a museum. Visiting this museum several times brought me a sense of closure I had been seeking for years. Genoa, with its beautiful views of the sea and mountains, became a place of peace for me. We often had picnic lunches next to the old ruins of the St. Andrea Cloister, surrounded by the city's beauty and history.

Looking back, I am struck by how resilient we were. Despite the challenges, we found strength in the kindness of strangers and the beauty around us. Our experiences taught me the importance of compassion, empathy, and perseverance. They shaped me into the person I am today.

My story is about resilience and the human capacity to overcome adversity. It reminds me that even in the darkest times, there am always hoping and a way forward. As I continue on my journey, I carry the lessons I learned with me, grateful for the strength and courage that have brought me this far. As I look to the future, I do so with optimism, knowing that no matter what challenges come my way, I have the resilience to face them head-on.

CHAPTER TEN

HOME OF THE FREE AND THE BRAVE

"I think of a hero as someone who understands the degree of responsibility that comes with their freedom."

— *BOB DYLAN*

A TRIP TO AMERICA

Mom corresponded with her family regularly, finding solace in their letters. Each one was a lifeline, a reminder that despite the vast distance separating us, we were not truly alone. Occasionally, a surprise would arrive in the mail—American dollars, a tangible promise of the new life awaiting us. These small but meaningful gestures reinforced our belief that our dreams were within reach, thanks to the unwavering support of family and the kindness of others.

Our journey to America was a testament to the resilience of our family and the hopes of countless immigrants before us. With the support of our Aunt Helen, who believed in us wholeheartedly, our voyage was made possible by a Jewish organization that funded our passage. This generous aid transformed our dream of a fresh start into a reality. Two years after we arrived, my mother fully repaid the debt, a symbol of our sacrifices and the new opportunities that lay ahead.

Los Angeles, 1966

The immigration process was difficult, filled with delays and setbacks. We faced a maze of bureaucracy and red tape as Mom had to request our documents from Israel and submit them to the American consulate. The situation was further complicated when my stepdad left behind our birth certificates. Retrieving them took a grueling year, filled with moments of uncertainty and doubt. Yet, through it all, my mom's determination never wavered. Her belief in a better future for us kept her moving forward, even when hope seemed distant.

As the day finally arrived for us to leave Italy, we gathered our belongings and said our goodbyes. We said goodbye to our school friends, our amazing teachers, and the neighbors who had shown us so much kindness. Mom's eyes welled up with tears of joy and relief as she saw her dreams coming to fruition. The tears were not just of sadness for leaving behind the familiar, but of happiness for the new beginnings that awaited us in America. It was a poignant moment of pure joy, knowing that all the struggles and hardships had led us to this point.

Through our family's journey, I learned profound lessons about perseverance, hope, and the power of community. Despite the formidable challenges we faced, we never gave up. We clung to our belief in a better future, and that belief carried us through even the toughest times. It's a lesson I carry with me today, forever grateful for the strength and resilience that guided us to where we are now.

UNITED STATES OF AMERICA, 1966

The day of departure finally arrived, a day we had dreamed of for so long. The thought of new beginnings and endless opportunities in the United States filled us with excitement. We were eager to reunite with our grandparents and extended family, and the joy of that prospect lifted our spirits. With passports and visas in hand, we were ready to embark on this life-changing journey.

Closing the apartment door in Via Lugo for the last time was bittersweet. We were leaving behind not just our home but also the memories of laughter, tears, and everyday moments that had become part of our lives. Yet, the excitement of what lay ahead outweighed the sadness. America, a land that had seemed so distant, was now within our grasp, offering a world of possibilities.

For the first time, our family, including my stepdad, boarded an airplane. The experience was a mix of excitement and raw nerves. Sitting by the window, I gazed out at the blue sky dotted with white clouds that looked like soft marshmallows. The peaceful view outside contrasted with the noisy airplane's engines, but I focused on the beauty of the sky, letting it calm my nerves.

This was more than just a trip—it was the beginning of a new life, full of unknowns and opportunities; adventures awaited me in this new land. Growing up, I had always heard of America as the greatest country on earth, a place where dreams could come true. Now, I was about to find out for myself.

My love for the English language added to my excitement. At home, we spoke Arabic, French, Hebrew, and Italian, but now I had the chance to speak, read, and write in English and learn Spanish. The challenge thrilled me, and I couldn't wait to dive into this new language, culture, and community. It felt like the opportunity I had been waiting for, and I was ready to embrace it.

As our plane approached the United States, I marveled at the vast expanse of clouds and the tiny houses below. The view was breathtaking. The captain's voice crackled over the intercom, announcing an emergency landing in Boston, Massachusetts. It was a slight detour, but after seven hours, we boarded another plane bound for New York. As we descended, the Statue of Liberty came into view. Although I didn't fully understand its significance then, I knew it symbolized something important—the promise of freedom for all who arrived on these shores.

Years later, when my oldest daughter graduated from junior high, we took a trip to New York City. One of the highlights was visiting the Statue of Liberty. As we climbed the spiral staircase to the crown, I was overwhelmed with emotion. Standing at the top, looking out at the sea, I was reminded of that first glimpse of the statue from the plane so many years before. It was a powerful moment, one that brought our journey full circle and deepened my appreciation for the life we had built in America.

Riding in a cab for the first time, I was captivated by the bustling streets of Manhattan. The skyscrapers seemed to touch the sky, and the yellow taxis lined up like soldiers, ready to ferry passengers through the city's vibrant streets. The energy was electric, unlike anything I had ever experienced. The city pulsed with life, and I was swept up in its rhythm.

Our hotel on the Upper East Side was old and charming. As we entered our room, my siblings and I couldn't contain our excitement. We jumped on the beds, laughing and shouting with joy. The television, broadcasting in English, was a novelty we had never experienced before. We didn't understand the language, but that didn't matter. The pure delight of watching cartoons without having to bribe anyone was a luxury we savored. That night, with the TV glowing and the promise of a new beginning in this land of endless possibilities, we felt a sense of joy and hope we hadn't felt in a long time.

The next morning, we boarded a plane bound for Los Angeles, California. Landing at Los Angeles International Airport was a mix of excitement and anxiety. As we stepped into the bustling terminal, my heart raced with anticipation. Meeting our aunt for the first time was emotional; my mom's face lit up as she embraced her older sister after so many years apart. The ride to our grandparents' apartment on Eighth Street was filled with stories and laughter, making up for lost time.

When we arrived, the entire extended family greeted us with warmth and love. Tears of happiness flowed as we were enveloped in their embrace. My mom was finally home, surrounded by relief, comfort, and joy. It was a moment that left a lasting impression on all of us.

The following day, my aunt and I went shopping at the nearby May Company department store. The bustling aisles were filled with bright colors and new clothes. I remember picking out knee-high socks and crisp white tennis shoes. The experience was exciting, a small but important step into my new life. The smell of new clothes and the bright lights of the store filled me with a sense of wonder and possibility. This simple shopping trip marked the beginning of many new adventures in our new country.

My aunt's unwavering support guided us through every step of our new life, from finding the right apartment to navigating the complexities of living in a new country. Her wisdom and love were a constant source of strength, reminding us that we were not alone in this journey. Each day brought new lessons and experiences, gradually helping us build our new life in America.

Looking back, those early years in Los Angeles are a testament to our family's strength and determination. We left behind everything we knew, including the familiar comforts of our old life, and in doing so, we discovered something profoundly beautiful—a place to call home and the freedom to shape our own destiny. Each hardship we overcame and every small victory we celebrated wove together into the rich tapestry of our new life. Sometimes, when I think about those days, I am moved to tears, remembering the overwhelming joy and relief of finally being home. Despite the world's shifting perspectives on America, my heart holds a steadfast truth: to me and my family, this land will always be the beacon of hope and the sanctuary that welcomed us with open arms. It is a place where dreams are born, possibilities are endless, and every struggle has led to the greatest gift of all—a home.

CHAPTER ELEVEN

WHEN I GROW UP...

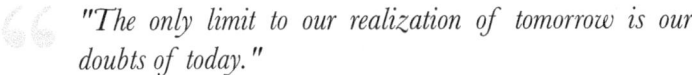

"The only limit to our realization of tomorrow is our doubts of today."

— *FRANKLIN D. ROOSEVELT*

WHAT DO YOU WANT TO BE WHEN YOU GROW UP?

Growing up as the oldest of sixteen siblings was a tumultuous journey. Our family dynamics were complex, filled with dysfunction, chaos, and a constant struggle to find our place. My mom had two sons and two daughters; I was the eldest, while my dad had ten sons and two daughters. The weight of expectations was heavy, and I often felt undervalued and misunderstood. There was constant pressure to excel, to lead by example, and to navigate the intricate family dynamics with strength and grace.

Despite the challenges, I yearned for freedom—to spread my wings and make my own mistakes. My self-esteem was so fragile that I could hardly envision anyone showing interest in me. I often felt invisible, overshadowed by the expectations and demands placed upon me. Rather than seeking personal validation or support, I focused intensely on my studies, driven by the need to prove myself and meet the high standards set for me. My self-worth seemed inextricably linked to my ability to excel academically and support my siblings, leaving little room for personal affirmation.

Whenever I fell short of these expectations, a deep sense of inadequacy would wash over me. I would blame myself for any failures, convinced that any misstep was a reflection of my own deficiencies. This self-blame only deepened my frustration and anger, creating a cycle of disappointment that was difficult to escape. In this environment, where the pressure to perform was relentless and the validation scarce, recognizing and appreciating my own worth became nearly impossible. The weight of unmet expectations and my internal struggles made it exceedingly hard to cultivate a sense of self-respect or to feel valued for who I truly was.

As I transitioned from childhood to adulthood, the experiences of my earlier years profoundly influenced my decision-making. Always a people-pleaser, I had to learn to set boundaries and say "no" when necessary. This lesson, though hard-won through hardship and pain, was pivotal for my personal growth. I longed to break free from the cycle of constantly trying to meet others' expectations and sought instead to empower those around me to carve their own paths.

Since I was thirteen, family members would often pose the daunting question, "What do you want to be when you grow up?" To them, success was synonymous with wealth, stability, and power. I frequently found myself at a loss for words, unable to articulate a response that aligned with their expectations.

Today, I see similar pressures imposed on children, including my own kindergarten-aged grandchildren. At a recent school performance, they were asked about their future aspirations. It saddened me to see how society tends to define children by their projected professions, often overlooking their current needs for security, love, and stability. Yet, when my youngest grandchild was asked about his future, he proudly declared he wanted to be a Ghostbuster. The audience erupted in laughter, but his innocent and imaginative response is exactly the sense of wonder I hope to nurture in my family. It's a reminder of the pure joy and creativity that should be celebrated and preserved, rather than overshadowed by the weight of societal expectations.

Perhaps these questions stem from a desire to live vicariously through our children, to fulfill unmet dreams through them. But it begs the question: what truly defines success? For me, success is about being a pillar of support, connecting with others, and fostering peace within my community. It's about finding happiness and love, staying positive, and empowering those around me—both in my family and in the broader community.

Through social networks and personal interactions, I strive to guide, encourage, and teach others to be fair and authentic. I believe in staying active and inspiring others to become the best versions of themselves. Life is a precious gift, and our actions negative or positive leave a ripple effect on those around us. Who are we to judge others' paths? Life is a journey, full of ups and downs.

My mantra is simple: do what you love, pursue your dreams, and embrace your passions. Understand your purpose and let it guide you. Success is not measured by wealth or status but by the impact we have on others and the fulfillment we find in our own lives. Follow your heart, both personally and professionally, and strive to leave the world a better place.

For many years, derailed dreams were a personal struggle. My life took a different course when I landed a part-time teller job in the banking industry. Though it wasn't my dream job, it reignited a spark I had long forgotten—my passion for art and interior design, a dream I had once written about in my journal.

I've learned that failure is not the end, but rather a valuable life lesson and a stepping stone for growth. My past circumstances do not define who I am today; I refuse to blame my upbringing. In fact, I am grateful for all my experiences, as they have shaped me into who I am. They provided me with the tools to change, grow, and empower others.

It has taken me seventy-one years to realize that the only opinion that truly matters is my own. I've learned to prioritize my happiness and fulfillment above all else. I no longer seek to control or judge others. I believe that everyone has the capacity to rise from rock bottom if they choose to. Success, to me, is not about avoiding failure but about embracing it, learning from it, and bouncing back stronger each time.

My journey is far from over; there are still many mountains to climb and dreams to pursue. I aspire to leave a legacy that inspires and empowers others, demonstrating resilience and perseverance through life's challenges. I am deeply grateful for every blessing in my life and remain steadfast in recognizing my own worth.

In my early years, by a house in Israel, I watched a vibrant pomegranate tree grow—a symbol of joy during my challenging childhood and young adulthood in the United States. Now, in the home where I've raised my children and welcomed grandchildren, the pomegranate tree continues to stand as a testament to our enduring spirit.

This tree links our past to the present, infusing warmth and life into our family home. It serves as a constant reminder of our roots and the perseverance that defines us. As we gather beneath its branches, the pomegranate tree embodies the resilience and vitality that flow through our family's veins.

1966 LOS ANGELES

Just a few weeks after our arrival in Los Angeles, my stepdad landed a job at the bustling movie studios in Burbank. His enthusiasm for his new role was palpable, and the cama-raderie with his coworkers seemed to bring a fresh spark to his days. During the holidays, employees were given turkeys, a quirky tradition that struck me as both peculiar and heart-warming.

Every morning, he would prepare sandwiches to sell at work, bringing a lighthearted spirit to his job. His laughter, once a bright and infectious presence in our home, soon dimmed when he was unexpectedly let go. The sudden loss cast a heavy shadow over the cheerfulness he had brought into our lives, leaving us to grapple with the uncertainty that followed.

Meanwhile, I enrolled at Bancroft Junior High for the final stretch of my 8th-grade year. Thrust into a new environment, I immersed myself in my studies, driven by a relentless deter-mination to master English. However, adjusting to life in Los Angeles proved to be an overwhelming challenge. The city's fast-paced lifestyle left me feeling isolated, awkward, and out of place.

My co-ed physical education class was a battleground of insecurities. I was ridiculed for being slightly overweight and for not adhering to the beauty standards of the time, such as shaving my legs and armpits. The taunts and sneers from my classmates felt like a constant assault, chipping away at my self-esteem. Each taunt was a reminder of how different I was, how I didn't quite fit in with the crowd. These experiences made it difficult to create connections, and I often felt like an outsider, struggling to find my place.

Despite the harsh treatment, I channeled my energy into my studies. I became more determined to excel academically, driven by a passion for learning that no one could take away from me. To escape the daily torment, I began taking an earlier bus to school, hoping to avoid the worst of the ridicule. After school, I walked home, returning my bus fare to my mom, knowing it would ease our financial strain. This small act of contribution provided me with a sense of purpose and a way to support her during our struggles.

One of the few sanctuaries I found was in my ESL English class. It was a haven for immigrants like me, each of us bringing our own unique stories and struggles. The classroom buzzed with a diverse array of faces and accents, all united by a shared determination to master English. Our teacher, Mr. Blackman, was a beacon of hope. Tall, with an olive complexion and an engaging presence, he brought the lessons to life with his wit and charisma. I was captivated by him, and like many teenagers, I harbored a secret crush, daydreaming of a future where I might marry someone like him.

Each lesson in Mr. Blackman's class felt like a step closer to understanding not just the language, but also my place in this new world. His enthusiasm was infectious, igniting a similar passion within me. Those mornings in ESL English were more than just academic sessions; they were a journey of self-discovery and connection, providing me with a glimmer of hope amid the difficulties.

As time passed, the initial fear and uncertainty gave way to a sense of belonging. My experiences at Bancroft Junior High School became a period of growth and self-discovery. I made friends, learned new things, and began to envision a future full of possibilities. The journey that began with a flight across the ocean was unfolding into a story of resilience, love, and the relentless pursuit of dreams.

CHAPTER TWELVE
THE APARTMENT BUILDING

 "All great changes are preceded by chaos."

— DEEPAK CHOPRA

SPAULDING AVENUE, 1966-1967

Our aunt helped us find an apartment in the Fairfax area in Los Angeles. The area was close to schools and within walking distance of local Eastern markets, offering a mix of familiar comforts and new experiences. The renters and their families were diverse, creating a vibrant community.

The seasons in Los Angeles each brought their own challenges. Summers were blisteringly hot, with the relentless sun beating down on us, while winters brought a cold that seeped into our small apartment. We huddled together on the small couch for warmth, finding comfort in each other's presence. Our apartment on Spaulding Avenue became our home from 1966 to 1967. Despite the difficulties, we found joy in simple things—playing games, sharing stories, and dreaming about the future.

Spaulding Avenue

Our new home was in the noisiest, most chaotic, and poorly managed four-unit apartment building in the neighborhood. The building was rundown and in need of major renovations. Our two-bedroom apartment, located on the second floor, had a small kitchen and one bathroom. The uncarpeted wood floors were cold and bare. A few months after moving in, I noticed some old, discarded carpet remnants in the back alley of a nearby carpet store. I managed to drag them home and cover the living room floor. Though the carpet was old and stained, it brought us a little warmth and a sense of comfort.

Our apartment building, though loud and sometimes chaotic, stood in stark contrast to the tranquility of the neighboring buildings. Life in our building was challenging, and as the oldest teenager, I often felt lonely and disconnected, retreating into my own world. In the small bedroom shared by my two younger siblings, I sought solace and escape from the chaos around us.

Directly across from us on the second floor lived an Italian family from New York. Maria, a stay-at-home mother of three, became a close friend to my mom. She frequently stopped by in the early morning, bringing us jelly donuts. The aroma of freshly brewed coffee filled our small kitchen as we shared our lives. Maria patiently helped my mom practice English, her kindness making our transition into this new world a bit easier.

These simple moments created a sense of belonging. Our small, imperfect apartment became a place of laughter and friendship. Despite the chaos and challenges, it was during these early years that we found a true sense of home and community. Our tiny living room was always filled with our extended family and a few of my mom's friends. The room buzzed with a mix of languages—Tunisian, Hebrew, French, and English—creating a lively and welcoming atmosphere. The doors were always open, inviting everyone in.

Her husband was less engaged with the neighbors, often retreating to their apartment after work. Sadly, their stay in California was short-lived. The 1971 earthquake struck the densely populated area of Los Angeles, prompting them to hurriedly move back to the East Coast. Their absence left a noticeable void in our lives, and over the years, we gradually lost touch. Decades later, they visited California again, but the reunion was bittersweet. Maria was very ill and soon passed away. Tragically, their two older children succumbed to drug addiction and also passed away. Only the youngest survived and is thriving in New York.

Below us, on the first floor, lived an elderly couple with their teenage daughter. Frequent loud arguments echoed through the building, painting a picture of a dysfunctional household. The parents were very strict disciplinarians, controlling their daughter's every move. I felt sorry for her. She often sought refuge in our apartment, spending most afternoons with us. She was the same age as my younger sister, and they quickly became close friends.

At seventeen, Margaret left her oppressive home environment, married her boyfriend, and started a family of her own. She had three children, but her life was marked by hardship. It was heartbreaking to learn that she became very ill later in life and faced significant financial struggles.

Directly across from them lived a single mom with three children and a brother who was a recovering alcoholic and unemployed. Life was a constant struggle. The oldest son, a troubled teen, dropped out of high school and eventually met a tragic end. One day, he broke into a local store, which caught fire. Unable to escape in time, he died at just sixteen years old. His death left a profound impact on the family and the remaining younger siblings, who eventually moved on with their lives.

Despite Jane's hardships, she remained resilient and devoted to her family. She had a deep love for the many cats that made their home with her. To make ends meet, she worked tirelessly as a server at Hollywood Studios, often arriving home late and leaving her children to fend for themselves. Despite her struggles, she created a warm and festive holiday atmosphere for her family. Her kindness extended beyond her own family. When we moved away, she continued to send handwritten greeting cards, a small gesture that spoke volumes about her character. Sadly, she passed away, leaving behind a legacy of hard work, kindness, and unwavering dedication to her family.

At one point, twelve kids and their families lived in our building, along with additional neighborhood kids who would play in front and in the back. Our playground was the cracked cement floor and overgrown weeds, a stark contrast to the manicured lawns of the surrounding neighborhood. We were the outcasts, but in our eyes, it was a place of freedom and adventure.

As we played, we would wait for cars to pass by and then resume chasing each other and playing ball once they were gone. The sound of laughter and shouts filled the air, masking the realities of our surroundings. Despite our circumstances, we found joy in the simplest things, creating memories that would stay with us for a lifetime.

Adjacent to our building was a similar apartment owned by an immigrant couple from Poland. The matriarch of the family often displayed a strong distaste toward our building and the families that lived in it. She was loud and angry, frequently warning us to stay away from her property. Her attitude served as a stark reminder of the divide between us and the rest of the neighborhood. Despite her animosity, we continued to play and make the most of our humble surroundings, finding comfort in each other's company.

The daily ritual of the Polish woman sweeping her driveway became familiar, yet she lacked a maternal instinct. Her yelling in her native language sent shivers down our spines. Her disapproval of our joyful antics was clear, but our laughter continued to fill the neighborhood, a testament to our resilience and spirit.

A SHATTERED IMAGE

My mother's depression escalated rapidly, a silent struggle that consumed her happiness. She became increasingly withdrawn with my stepfather, her every breath heavy with unspoken despair. It was a gradual erosion of the vibrant woman I once knew, replaced by a shadow of sadness. The day it all became too much is seared into my memory, a nightmare that still haunts me.

One afternoon, the air in our apartment felt suffocating with dread. My mom retreated to the bathroom, locking the door behind her. At first, it seemed like another attempt to find solitude, but then the cries began—cries of a tormented soul, a heart breaking beyond repair. The sound pierced the air, filling me with fear and sorrow.

I stood outside the door, pounding on it, my voice joining

her cries in a desperate attempt to reach her. My stepfather, sensing the urgency, rushed over and kicked the door in. Inside, the scene was one of horror. My mother sat on the cold, tiled floor, slumped forward, with one of her wrists slashed and blood pooling around her.

This once vibrant woman, the heart of our family, was now undone by the weight of despair. I stood there, paralyzed by shock, my mind struggling to process the grim reality before me. Time seemed to stretch, every second an eternity. I wanted to scream, to cry, to do anything to release the torment tearing through me, but I couldn't. Instead, a part of me took over. I forced myself to act, to stop the bleeding. I grabbed kitchen towels, pressing them against her wrist, my hands trembling with fear and determination. My stepfather was beside me, his face a mask of terror and helplessness. Together, we worked in silence; trying to hold on to the woman we loved.

In the chaos, our neighbor next door called the paramedics, who arrived just in time. Their swift actions were a blur as they took over, their calmness in stark contrast to the turmoil inside me. They stabilized my mother and rushed her to the hospital. My father and I followed in silence, the drive a journey through tears.

Miraculously, my mother survived, but the scars of that day—both physical and emotional—remained. Looking back, the image of my mother in that bathroom is etched in my mind. She was a strong woman who raised four children under difficult circumstances. In the years that followed, with the help of therapy and medication, she found some peace and the strength to divorce my stepfather and move on with her life.

This tragedy is a reminder of the fragility of the human spirit and the need for understanding and compassion in the face of mental illness. My mother's struggles are a testament to the silent battles many face, often unnoticed until it's too late. As we move forward, one day at a time, we carry the weight of that memory but also the hope of healing and resilience. My mother remains in my mind, reminding me of her strength and our enduring love.

CHAPTER THIRTEEN

A PARTY DRESS AND MILITARY DUFFLE

 "The measure of who we are is what we do with what we have."

— *VINCE LOMBARDI*

THE JEWISH AMERICAN PRINCESS

I was invited to my next-door neighbor Ingrid's sweet sixteen party, a rare opportunity to glimpse into a world that seemed both distant and alluring. Although we were never really friends, the invitation was a pleasant surprise, and I was genuinely excited to attend.

There was just one problem—I had nothing to wear. Desperate, I borrowed a dress from another neighbor and felt a sense of transformation as I slipped it on. We arrived at the party in her dad's 1957 Chevy, cruising down Sunset Blvd. to a restaurant bathed in a dim, romantic glow. As we stepped inside, I couldn't help but notice that many of the guests were much older, with only a handful of her peers present. It was a stark contrast to the glamorous image of a typical sweet sixteen party, and I felt a pang of sadness for her.

Ingrid was the embodiment of what the neighborhood called a "JAP," or Jewish American Princess. Tall and slender, she always seemed impeccably dressed, radiating a life of ease and luxury that I could only dream of. Despite our different worlds, I hoped this party might be the beginning of a meaningful friendship between us.

On the way home, Ingrid was lively and engaging, sparking a glimmer of hope in me. I believed that perhaps this could be the start of something special, a friendship that transcended our differences. Unfortunately, that hope was short-lived.

The closest I ever came to experiencing a world of luxury and beauty was through my job at the local May Company clothing department store during the annual inventory, when I was fourteen. Although I couldn't afford any of the beautiful clothes, simply touching and admiring them was a rare treat. We worked late into the night, counting inventory with small pencils and pads, and earned a modest $5.25 in cash. It was a fleeting glimpse into a world that felt tantalizingly close yet still so far away.

As I moved away from Southern California, I made frequent visits to my mom, often driving back to Spaulding Avenue. Each visit was a reminder of our past and the journey we had undertaken. Our old apartment building, once a symbol of struggle, had transformed into a desirable residence in a sought-after neighborhood.

One day, I hope to knock on that old apartment door, walk through its familiar halls, and touch its walls, each surface holding a story from our life long ago. These thoughts fill me with gratitude and humility, reminding me of the blessings that have come my way and the journey that has shaped me into who I am today.

1967: FOURTEEN YEARS OLD

Summertime arrived, and with it came thrilling news—a two-week scholarship to a summer camp in Big Bear, California, courtesy of the Jewish Community Center. I had never been away from home before, so the prospect of exploring the mountains, trying my hand at camping, and hopefully making a few new friends was both exhilarating and nerve-wracking.

In the days leading up to the trip, I was given a list of items to pack: clothes, toiletries, and other essentials. Given my minimal wardrobe, I felt a pang of anxiety. I turned to my neighbor for help, and she generously lent me her husband's military duffle bag. I stuffed my entire wardrobe into it—two pairs of shorts, a couple of tops, a single pair of tennis shoes, and a small jacket—hoping it would be enough. The bag looked like it had seen better days, with its faded green canvas and a faint smell of old leather, but it was my ticket to adventure.

The day of departure arrived, and I eagerly boarded the camp bus, joining a group of teenagers who were just as excited as I was. The two-hour ride to the mountain campground was filled with chatter and laughter, but my nerves were a bundle of jangling nerves. As we pulled into the camp, my eyes widened at the sight of the camp staff, who greeted us with enthusiastic waves and broad smiles. They quickly assigned us to our cabins, and I could barely contain my excitement as I envisioned the adventures that awaited us.

The cabin we were assigned to had six bunk beds, arranged in two neat rows. My bunkmates, who had clearly come prepared, began unpacking their belongings from large, colorful suitcases, chatting animatedly as they did so. I stood there with my old army duffle bag, trying to fit in while feeling like a misplaced puzzle piece. I had only five minutes to unpack, which felt like a lifetime. Amid their laughter and stories, I felt painfully out of place, my simple outfits and worn shoes contrasting sharply with their trendy gear.

The days at camp were a whirlwind of activities. One evening, a dance was organized in the activity hall. Having never danced a slow dance before, I approached the experience with a mix of curiosity and trepidation. My dance partner, a young man with a nervous smile, held me tightly as we swayed to the music. His cheek brushed against mine, and while it was meant to be romantic, it felt awkward and strangely intimate. I found myself longing for the dance to end so I could escape his tight grasp and reclaim my personal space.

One of the highlights of the camp was a group outing to Lake Arrowhead. However, this too brought its own set of challenges. While the other girls splurged on souvenirs and snacks, I found myself standing on the sidelines, feeling like an outsider. My empty hands and lack of funds made me feel even more isolated. Overwhelmed and homesick, I called my mom in tears, begging her to let me come home early. It was one of those moments where you wish you could crawl into a small hole and disappear, but instead, you wait out the minutes, hour by hour, until the week finally drags its way to an end.

As the departure day finally arrived, I said my goodbyes with a mixture of relief and sadness. The camp had been a place of challenges, discomfort, and moments of awkwardness, but it had also been a crucible of self-discovery. Despite the discomfort, I had learned the valuable lesson of finding comfort in my own skin and accepting that it was okay to feel out of place sometimes. As I left behind the camp and its well-meaning counselors, I carried with me the realization that even uncomfortable experiences could shape us in meaningful ways.

FAIRFAX HIGH SCHOOL

Fairfax High School, affectionately dubbed "the Jewish high school," thrived amidst a predominantly Jewish neighborhood, where many residents were second or third-generation immigrants. During the 1960s and 1970s, it was a hub of linguistic diversity, serving as a foreign language magnet school. From Chinese and Latin to German, French, and Hebrew, the school offered a rich array of languages that reflected the vibrant cultural mosaic of its student body.

For me, Fairfax was more than just a school; it was a gateway to endless opportunities. Already fluent in several languages, I was determined to perfect my skills, particularly in writing. Hebrew, Italian, French, Arabic, and Spanish were not mere subjects but integral parts of my daily life. My grandmother, with her remarkable ability to blend three languages into a single sentence, was a testament to the multilingual environment that shaped my upbringing.

Founded in 1924, our school's campus had once been a splendid example of Spanish Colonial Revival architecture. However, by 1966, most of the campus had to be demolished to meet earthquake safety standards. The rotunda, a grand remnant of our school's storied past, survived. It became the stage for memorable concerts featuring artists like Eddie Albert and the Tijuana Brass, and the Fifth Dimension, whose hit "The Age of Aquarius" reverberated far beyond our school's walls.

During my years at Fairfax from 1964 to 1970, we were led by Principal Jim Tunney. Little did we know, he was not just an educational leader but a former NFL referee with a remarkable record of 29 postseason assignments, including ten championship games and Super Bowls. Meeting him personally was a privilege that added an unexpected layer of excitement to our school experience.

Education was my beacon, guiding me toward the American dream. Yet, high school was fraught with its own set of challenges. My teenage years were marked by the turbulence of adolescence—hormones raging, acne marring my skin, and the financial strain on my family amplifying the chaos at home. The echoes of my parents' arguments were a constant backdrop to my daily life.

In this whirlwind, the Hebrew, Italian, and French clubs became my sanctuary. The few friends I made, with backgrounds and experiences similar to mine, offered a sense of solidarity. One memorable moment of connection came when a shy Hispanic boy, taller than me by three inches, asked me to the junior prom. As the date approached, my anxiety grew.

To my surprise, our neighbor and her friend transformed me into a Cinderella for the evening. I borrowed a dress that was a size too small, and though it felt tight and uncomfortable, the effort they put into making me feel special was touching. My hair, usually longer, was styled into a tight bun reminiscent of a Geisha. Despite my nerves, their kindness created a moment of magic amid the turmoil.

The high school cafeteria was magically transformed for the prom. Dim lighting and festive decorations turned it into a warm, glowing ballroom. The music filled the air, creating an atmosphere of elegance and enchantment that contrasted sharply with the usual bustle of the cafeteria. For that evening, surrounded by the soft glow of candlelight, I felt truly beautiful and happy. All my high school insecurities seemed to melt away, replaced by the pure joy of the moment.

Throughout high school, I remained single, never asked out and feeling my self-confidence at an all-time low. I watched enviously as other girls walked hand-in-hand with their boyfriends, while I stood on the sidelines, feeling like an outsider. The cheerleaders, with their confidence and exclusive aura, flaunted their uniforms and boyfriends' letterman jackets. Despite their seemingly aloof demeanor, one cheerleader was unexpectedly kind, greeting me with a nod in Algebra class. Years later, at our 25th reunion, I learned she had become a successful attorney and mother. Her kindness was a poignant reminder that high school, with all its complexities, was just a small chapter in our lives.

At the reunion, I found that many classmates didn't remember me, and I struggled to recall them as well. The gathering was a mix of highly successful individuals—actors, media personalities, attorneys, businesspeople, writers, and producers. Some were married or divorced, others single, perhaps searching for connections. The passage of time had changed many; the youth and beauty we once took for granted had faded.

High School Graduation

During high school, I often crossed paths with Jackie Jackson of the Jackson 5 fame. Despite being surrounded by so many classmates, I never truly connected with them, nor they with me. I didn't fit into the typical high school mold. Yet, I graduated with honors, though my graduation day was a solitary affair. My grandfather was my sole family member in attendance, and there were no flowers or fanfare, only a quiet moment of personal achievement.

Thirty years later, at our reunion, I was eager to reconnect. Our class, a shining example of resilience, had produced an impressive array of successful individuals. CEOs, attorneys, doctors, writers, and producers—our achievements were a testament to the determination and success that defined us.

CHAPTER FOURTEEN

KINGS ROAD 1966-1967

"The only way to make sense out of change is to plunge into it, move with it, and join the dance."

— ALAN WATTS

A NEW BEGINNING: KINGS ROAD

Two years after moving from Spaulding Avenue, we transitioned into a small two-bedroom, one-bath single-family home on Kings Road. This change coincided with my mother finalizing her divorce from my stepfather. His gambling addiction had spiraled out of control, and she had reached her breaking point. Back then, getting into rehab was difficult and prohibitively expensive, leaving little hope for his recovery.

My mother continued to work as a babysitter from our home, relying on welfare and food stamps assistance to make ends meet. Our new neighborhood was a mix of single-family homes and apartment buildings, but what I loved most was its proximity to the bustling streets of Santa Monica and Sunset Boulevards.

Not far from our home, the famous Laurel Canyon buzzed with counterculture activity. It became a haven for burgeoning musicians, with the homes of legends like Joni Mitchell, Jim Morrison, Carole King, and the Eagles turning into sanctuaries for artists of the time. The music world was shifting rapidly, faster than anyone could keep up.

The father of a school friend, who was in one of my high school clubs, was a music producer. He invited us to see Janis Joplin and her group, Big Brother and the Holding Company, perform at the Whisky a Go-Go. The line outside was long and winding, creating a surreal atmosphere. We were ushered into the small, dark club, every seat filled with an overflow of standing room only. The pungent smell of marijuana permeated the air, making me feel nauseated—a place I felt I didn't belong.

Janis took the stage, her beautiful, raspy voice filling the room. She was captivating, yet her appearance was disheveled. Despite this, her performance was unforgettable. My favorite song was "Me and Bobby McGee." Tragically, just a week after this mesmerizing performance, she was found dead from a heroin overdose. The news was heartbreaking.

The Whisky a Go-Go was a legendary venue, hosting many iconic artists like Jimi Hendrix, The Byrd's, and Buffalo Springfield. It played a crucial role in the careers of many Southern California bands.

A TOUCH OF GLAMOUR AND A SLICE OF REALITY

After graduating from high school, a few friends and I would hang out by the country store in Laurel Canyon, Micheli's Pizza. Occasionally, some of these legendary musicians would stop by to order food and hang out. Seeing them in such a casual setting added a touch of magic to our ordinary days.

Laurel Canyon, along with Sunset and Santa Monica

Boulevards, was not just a place; it was the heartbeat of a transformative era. Many afternoons, I looked forward to the live variety shows at CBS Studios. The contrast between the glitzy, star-studded world of variety shows and the creative energy of the music scene made my teenage years unforgettable.

In 1970, Kenny Loggins released "Danny's Song," a track that resonated deeply with me. Its lyrics were both poignant and uplifting: "Even though we ain't got money, I'm so in love with you, honey, and everything will bring a chain of love." Those words echoed my own hopes and dreams, promising that love would make everything alright.

MENTORS AND MEMORIES

Donna, whose daughter my mom babysat, became a close family friend. She worked for the William Morris Agency and often invited me to concerts and backstage events. I had the incredible opportunity to meet artists Joan Baez, Gordon Lightfoot, John Denver, and the Beach Boys. These experiences were unforgettable, yet the contrast between the glamorous world of music and the harsh realities of addiction and loss lingered heavily in my mind.

We lived a few minutes from CBS Studios, making it easy to attend tapings of my favorite variety shows, such as The Sonny and Cher Show and The Carol Burnett Show. I became a regular, always finding my way to the front row, close to the stage. It was a delightful way to pass a few afternoons, lost in laughter and entertainment.

On my second trip to Paris, France, we visited Jim Morrison's grave at Père Lachaise Cemetery. He was the most iconic entertainer of his time, and standing by his final resting place felt surreal and poignant.

THE IMPACT OF YVETTE

My sister and I were paired with volunteers from the Big Brother Big Sister organization, a group dedicated to supporting children's mental health and emotional development. One day, a young woman introduced herself to me. She seemed barely older than I was—short in stature but big in heart. This was Yvette, who would become not just a mentor but a cherished member of our family.

Yvette, a UCLA student, lived in a cozy one-bedroom apartment near the campus. Despite being an only child, she embraced the chaos of our large extended family. Her parents owned a chicken farm in Connecticut, a detail that never failed to intrigue me. Despite the ten-year age gap, Yvette and I quickly formed a deep bond.

She became my guide to the world beyond, taking me along to her college classes. I was enthralled by the lively interactions of the students and the vibrant atmosphere of campus life. Yvette was not just a mentor; she was a confidant, a friend who understood me in ways others couldn't. Our relationship was a lifeline for both of us, a source of comfort and strength in a world that often felt confusing and overwhelming.

Through Yvette, I found a sense of belonging and purpose. She became part of our family, attending gatherings and celebrations with us. Her presence brought joy and stability to my life, reminding me that even in the midst of uncertainty, there are people who care deeply for us.

Yvette's impact on my life was profound. She taught me the value of kindness and compassion, of reaching out to others in need. She showed me that family is not just about blood relations but about the bonds we form with those who touch our lives in meaningful ways. She will always hold a special place in my heart.

JOYFUL MOMENTS WITH SHIMON

One of our family friends, Shimon, and his wife, Joy, often stopped by our apartment. We took turns visiting each other, sharing stories and laughter. Joy made coffee while Shimon launched into his joke routines. The laughter began the minute we walked in, his preferred languages of Hebrew and Arabic weaving through his hilarious anecdotes.

We would crack up, one joke after another, unable to contain our laughter. Shimon was a poor man, but he was rich in spirit. His humor and warmth made everyone eager to spend time with him. Sometimes, people with lots of money seem bored and have little to share, but those without wealth, like Shimon, are often filled with laughter and a genuine joy in the company of others. It's a true gift.

Those moments in our tiny living room, with laughter bouncing off the walls, are some of my most cherished memories. They remind me that richness in life comes not from material wealth but from the love and joy we share with those around us.

CHAPTER FIFTEEN

THE NEXT-DOOR NEIGHBOR

 "Life is not about waiting for the storm to pass, but about learning how to dance in the rain."

— *VIVIAN GREENE*

A MAN NAMED FREDDIE

In the heart of our neighborhood lived a man named Freddie, a Southern gentleman with a voice as warm as the afternoon sun. When he moved in next door, he quickly became a familiar face. For my mom, who had endured two difficult marriages, Freddie was a comforting presence. After everything she had been through, it was a relief to see her smile again.

Freddie became more than just a neighbor; he became part of our family. His easygoing nature brought a sense of calm to our home, which had seen its share of turbulence. With Freddie around, our house felt warmer, filled with a new kind of peace.

Although I graduated with high honors from high school, I couldn't afford to attend university. Instead, I enrolled in junior college and landed a part-time job at a local bank. Amidst this turmoil, I found myself at a crossroads, not fulfilling my dreams. Despite quick promotions, I felt trapped, knowing deep down that banking wasn't my passion. I held onto the hope that one day, I would find my true calling.

CRESCENT HEIGHTS BLVD, LOS ANGELES 1969

Crescent Heights Blvd

Life seemed to take a turn for the better when we moved to Crescent Heights Blvd. My mom secured a job as a nurse's aide at a private hospital, often interacting with celebrities undergoing plastic surgery. While the job had its glamour, my mom was never one to be star-struck.

Freddie moved in with us, bringing a sense of stability. It felt like a fresh start, a chance for happiness to finally settle in. But as time passed, Freddie's drinking became a problem. What began as occasional drinks escalated, and it was clear that his health was steadily declining. Despite my mom's efforts to help him, Freddie's health continued to worsen, and eventually, he passed away. His death was a harsh reminder of life's fragility. Yet, despite his struggles, Freddie had brought joy into our lives, and we held onto those memories, grateful for the comfort he had provided during difficult times.

With the help of our aunt, we purchased our first home with a minimal down payment. Pooling our savings, we bought a 1,470-square-foot, two-bedroom, one-bathroom Spanish-style house built in 1947. My aunt helped us find it and facilitated our move. The house also included a small maid's quarters with its own bathroom.

The open space, with its high ceilings and wrought iron accents, was very impressive. Sunlight streamed through the elegant French windows, brightening the space and making it feel like home. Despite this new beginning, family life remained strained. My mom's disappointment from the constant battles with my stepdad and the additional financial support needed was always a topic of conversation. In spite of it all, our home was filled with our extended family and my mom's friends—a place where emotions ran high and every day was filled with a mix of angst, joy, and everything in between.

The tiny room that was once the maid's quarters became my oasis. The old washing machine nearby provided a comforting hum, a reminder of the life happening around me. To make the space feel more like mine, I bought a small white wicker desk from a flea market, placing it beneath the small French windows with lace curtains. It wasn't much, but it was my own little corner of the world.

Despite my busy schedule with school and work, I reconnected with old high school friends. We often met at Norm's Restaurant on La Cienega Blvd, sharing laughter and memories. My cousin Reine, just six months older than me, was a frequent companion. Whether we were hanging out at her apartment or exploring coffee houses on Santa Monica Blvd, she always made life feel lighter.

At work, I made new friends, especially among those who had recently migrated from Europe. We often gathered at The Athenian Gardens, a Greek restaurant and dance hall in Hollywood. The lively music and delicious Mediterranean food resonated with me in a way I couldn't explain. I later discovered that my biological dad and grandfather were both born in Salonica, Greece, deepening my connection to the culture and making those moments even more meaningful.

Weekends were spent in the vibrant energy of Westwood Village, mingling with UCLA students. We frequented local clubs around the campus, where live bands set the tone for unforgettable nights. The saxophonist's melodies were the highlight, though the pervasive smell of pot on the dance floor often made me feel uneasy. It was a time of rebellion, drugs, sex, and rock and roll, but I never saw myself as part of that scene.

Despite the temptations around me, I was always reminded of my role in the family as a role model to my siblings, the "good girl" who had to remain responsible. The pressure to be perfect weighed heavily on me. I wanted my mom to be proud, to see that even if I stumbled, it would be okay. But I was cautious, making decisions that wouldn't jeopardize my work or studies.

CHAPTER SIXTEEN

A DECADE OF CHANGE

 "It is not the strongest of the species that survive, nor the most intelligent, but the one most responsive to change."

— *CHARLES DARWIN*

1966- 1970: TURBULENT YEARS

Living on Crescent Heights Blvd., our home was a lively mix of chaos and camaraderie, constantly brimming with activity. My younger brother and sister had an unending fascination with animals, frequently bringing home stray cats and dogs despite my mother's protests. Although I wasn't particularly fond of these animals, their enthusiasm was contagious, and I often found myself swept up in their adventures.

One sweltering summer night, I struggled to find relief from the oppressive heat. Seeking a breeze, I decided to open the window in our back bedroom. The cool air that flowed in was a welcome relief, and I drifted off to sleep with a contented smile. However, my tranquility was short-lived. In the dead of night, I was abruptly awakened by a loud screeching sound. My heart raced as I sat up, bewildered by the noise. To my horror, a feral black cat had leaped through the open window and landed right beside me. I let out a piercing scream, which reverberated through the room.

The startled cat darted around, knocking over everything in its path. The commotion roused the entire household, and soon my parents and siblings were all in the room, trying to capture the elusive feline. My mother, who had always harbored a fear of cats, was frantically shouting instructions, adding to the pandemonium. Despite the fear and confusion, we were united in our effort to tackle this unexpected challenge. After what felt like an eternity, we finally managed to catch the cat and release it safely outside. As the adrenaline subsided, we collapsed onto the bed, laughing at the absurdity of the situation.

In the days that followed, the incident became a beloved family anecdote. We often recounted the night of the "Crescent Heights Cat Burglar" to friends and relatives, each retelling growing more embellished and humorous. Looking back, I realize that those chaotic, laughter-filled moments made our home on Crescent Heights truly special. Despite our modest living conditions and limited resources, we were rich in love and humor. And while I was never a fan of cats, that unexpected adventure taught me that sometimes the most memorable moments in life are the ones that catch us completely off guard.

On another occasion, I accompanied my younger siblings to our neighborhood public swimming pool, despite my own lack of swimming skills. I felt self-conscious and awkward, worried that other kids might ridicule my attempts. As I stood by the poolside, I envied the carefree joy of those diving into the water, especially my siblings, whose laughter rang out with every splash. Wrapped in a towel, I longed to join them, to experience that same sense of freedom and delight. Yet, my fear held me back, leaving me as a silent observer of their fun-filled adventures. Today, the vibrant pool has vanished, replaced by a mundane post office, serving as a stark reminder of the fleeting nature of childhood joy.

DAILY STRUGGLES

Our daily struggles were numerous. We relied on the welfare system to supplement my mom's income from babysitting infants in our cramped two-bedroom apartment. My dad, now unemployed, had taken up a new vice: the Hollywood horse races and various gambling halls around Los Angeles. His gambling addiction cast a dark shadow over our family, draining both our finances and our happiness.

Growing up, I often felt the weight of the world on my young shoulders. Our apartment, though filled with love, was also a constant reminder of our financial struggles. Mom worked tirelessly, often juggling multiple jobs to provide for us. Her strength and determination were nothing short of awe-inspiring, but the toll it took on her was evident.

As the oldest sibling, I felt a deep sense of responsibility for my younger brother and sister. I tried my best to shield them from the harsh realities of our life, though I knew they were not oblivious to our struggles. Despite the hardships, there were moments of joy and respite. I cherish the times when Mom would gather us around the table for a simple meal, and for those brief moments, all our worries would fade away.

As I grew older, the weight of our circumstances began to take its toll on me. I grappled with feelings of inadequacy and self-doubt, questioning if I would ever escape the cycle of poverty and addiction that plagued our family. It wasn't until I sought help through therapy and mentorship that I began to see a glimmer of hope.

Therapy allowed me to confront my past and recognize its impact on me. I learned that my worth wasn't defined by our circumstances but by the strength and resilience I had demonstrated in the face of adversity. It was a long and challenging journey, filled with tears and moments of despair, but it was also one of self-discovery and growth.

Today, I look back on those difficult years with a blend of sadness and gratitude. I feel sadness for the pain and suffering we endured, but also gratitude for the lessons learned and the strength gained. Our story is one of resilience and hope—a testament to the power of the human spirit to overcome even the darkest of times. While the scars of our past may never fully heal, they serve as a reminder of the strength and resilience that lies within each of us.

CHAPTER SEVENTEEN
FROM SMALL BEGINNINGS
TO BIG DREAMS

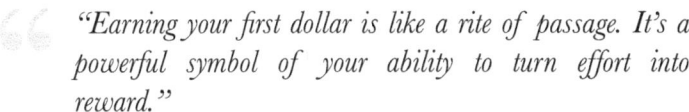

"Earning your first dollar is like a rite of passage. It's a powerful symbol of your ability to turn effort into reward."

— *UNKNOWN*

1967 LOS ANGELES WORK PORTFOLIO

My high school and college years were marked by a series of jobs that, while challenging, helped shape my career aspirations and clarified what I truly wanted in life.

My very first job involved babysitting two adorable children, aged four and six, for a single mother working in Hollywood. Her demanding job in an escort service required someone reliable to care for her kids, and I was that person. Every afternoon, she would pick me up, and I'd spend time with her children until the early morning. Despite her demanding profession, she was a kind and beautiful woman who deeply cared for her kids. Once the children were asleep, I would tidy up her small apartment on Fountain Avenue and clean the kitchen. For my efforts, I earned 50 cents an hour—a modest wage, but it felt like a treasure.

I worked for her for three months, and during that time, she showed immense kindness and appreciation, often leaving me sweet notes that expressed how much she valued my help. Earning $100 a month, with half given to my mom to supplement her income. I felt a surge of pride when I used my hard-earned money to buy new clothes for the first time. I headed downtown to the famous alley in Los Angeles, feeling like a million bucks. In 1969, a hundred dollars felt like a king's ransom, and I was incredibly proud of myself.

On weekends, I took on another job that was both challenging and rewarding. I worked for a blind man, helping with typing and light household duties. Communication was minimal, making the job a bit awkward at times, especially when I spent hours typing 4x5 cards. Yet, despite the challenges, I felt a sense of fulfillment in helping someone in need.

Living near the famous Farmers Market on Fairfax Avenue added a touch of excitement to my life. I landed a part-time job at Clara's Bread Bin kiosk, where we sold delicious desserts and specialty bread flown in daily from San Francisco. This bustling kiosk attracted tourists from around the world, and my multilingual skills—Hebrew, Arabic, Spanish, French, Italian, and now English—made me an invaluable asset to the Italian owner. When the market closed, I had made friends with most of the vendors, who treated me to leftover food and freshly squeezed juice. My mom never had to buy bread; we were gifted day-old loaves every night, so she ended up with five to six loaves a week.

Working at an international headhunter's agency, punching data into the NCR machine, was more than just a job—it was a dream factory where I envisioned traveling the world, living and working in different countries. But my dreams were dashed when the agency suddenly closed shortly after I was hired. I was heartbroken. The owner of the agency was a striking man—handsome, charismatic, and incredibly intelligent. A practicing Buddhist, he introduced me to Buddhism, which was foreign yet intriguing to me. His influence extended beyond the office, as he invited all the employees to his beautiful estate in the Hollywood Hills.

Stepping into his home was like entering a different world. The large living room was serene and quiet, mesmerizing me. Then, he began to chant and rang a tiny bell in a brass bowl, the sound reverberating through the room. A large Buddha sculpture greeted us in the entrance hall. As someone of the Jewish faith, the experience was both foreign and fascinating.

Outside of work, the hippie movement was in full swing on the streets of Los Angeles. Young adults flaunted hot pants, bell-bottom jeans, and beaded necklaces, while Tibetan monks dressed in bright orange chanted "Hare Krishna" as they walked down the streets. This vibrant cultural atmosphere sparked a deep curiosity in me. I wanted to learn more about religions and cultures different from my own. It was a time of exploration and discovery, filled with experiences that shaped my perspective on the world.

I then found myself in a design art studio nestled in West Los Angeles, surrounded by two dynamic clothing and jewelry designers. They were masters of their craft, creating beautiful classic cashmere and wool-blend dresses. Captivated by their knowledge and passion for design, I was guided through the intricate world of fashion transformation and creation.

They generously gifted me with their creations, which inspired my future journey into interior and exterior design. Although insecurities held me back from fully embracing my passions for years, life nudged me in the right direction. Eventually, I immersed myself in the fashion industry, interacting with clients and learning the ropes of the trade. It was an exhilarating journey, filled with challenges and triumphs, but through it all, I discovered the joy of unleashing my creative spirit. Many years later I created in designing beautiful jewelry.

Those days were marked by hard work, laughter, and unexpected friendships. They taught me the value of perseverance and the joy of making a difference in someone's life, no matter how small the gesture.

Picture a young woman, full of dreams and aspirations, working as a part-time teller at a local savings and loan company in Beverly Hills. This job was a stepping stone toward her dreams, a means to support herself while her husband built his import business and traveled to Europe. Despite her ambitions, her path was fraught with challenges. Her mother, in need of emotional and financial support, relied heavily on her. Nineteen years apart, she became her mother's source of strength, putting her own dreams on hold to be near her.

Yet, despite these challenges, she remained committed to excelling in her job. Her hard work paid off, advancing her to a supervisory position with a salary that met the demands of life in Beverly Hills. Surrounded by wealth and glamour, she encountered icons like Steve McQueen, Ali McGraw, Liza Minnelli, and Fred Astaire, each encounter a reminder of Hollywood's allure. Despite the glitz and glamour, she knew deep down that this world was not where she truly belonged.

Amidst it all, she remained grounded, returning home to her reality with her dreams still burning brightly in her heart. It was a time of growth, challenges overcome, and moments that would shape her path toward a future where her dreams would finally take flight.

Imagine reaching the pinnacle of success in your career, becoming a branch manager and vice president in the banking industry, and being slated to become a district branch manager. This moment of triumph, the culmination of seventeen years of hard work, patience, and perseverance, brings a realization that true success is not just in professional achievements but in the moments spent with loved ones, especially your children.

As you immerse yourself in parenthood, another passion emerges—history, antiques, and design. Each project in these fields brings a sense of fulfillment and joy. Additionally, the rich flavors and traditions of cooking connect you with your heritage. Drawing from recipes passed down by your grand-mother and mother, you embark on a culinary journey exploring North African/Mediterranean cuisine. It's a way to savor the flavors of your past while creating new memories with your family.

In this journey of self-discovery and reevaluation, one thing becomes clear—what we think is important today may not hold the same significance in the future. Life is ever-changing, and our goals and passions evolve with it. The key is to embrace these changes, savor each moment, and find happiness and success in doing what you love most.

CHAPTER EIGHTEEN

STRUGGLES AND BLESSINGS

"What lies behind us and what lies before us are tiny matters compared to what lies within us."

— *RALPH WALDO EMERSON*

CALIFORNIA AND THE WORLD CHANGING (1967)

In the late 1960s, Hollywood, California, was at the center of a cultural revolution. Mini dresses, hot pants, and the rise of sex, drugs, and rock and roll set the tone for an era that would leave a lasting impact. As the entertainment capital of the world, Hollywood mirrored the rapid transformations sweeping the nation, including my hometown of Los Angeles. The Vietnam War became a major catalyst for social change, sparking heated debates and widespread protests. These were tumultuous times, marked by the tragic assassinations of leaders like Martin Luther King Jr., President John F. Kennedy, and his brother Robert Kennedy, just twenty minutes from my home at the Roosevelt Hotel on Hollywood Blvd.

In high school I purchased a silver metal bracelet inscribed with the names of MIA soldiers—those missing in action—for $5.00. I wore that bracelet for over two years, a somber reminder of the human cost of war. The country was reeling, experiencing what many called a "cultural shock." People were divided; some opposed the Vietnam War and fled to Canada, while others embraced alternative lifestyles in communal settings, rejecting societal norms.

Songs like "If You're Going to San Francisco, Be Sure to Wear Flowers in Your Hair" captured the spirit of the times. Haight-Ashbury Street in San Francisco became synonymous with the counterculture movement, a place I longed to experience for myself. Decades later, when I finally visited, I found that the street had transformed into a trendy area, bustling with coffee houses, restaurants, art galleries, and clothing stores, yet still holding onto a hint of its storied past.

In Los Angeles, Santa Monica and Sunset Boulevards were alive with activity, especially at night. Numerous nightclubs and entertainment venues drew crowds, and the atmosphere was electric, filled with a sense of freedom and possibility. Young people sought to break free from societal expectations, carving out their own paths.

Looking back, those years were a blend of excitement, uncertainty, and hope. The world was changing, and we were caught in the midst of it, navigating the complexities of war, social upheaval, and personal growth. It was a time that shaped who I am today, reminding me of the importance of standing up for what you believe in, even when the world around you is in chaos.

BECOMING AN AMERICAN CITIZEN

In 1970, I took a pivotal step that would shape the course of my life. At just 18 years old, I stood alone amidst a sea of 1,000 other hopefuls in the grand, echoing halls of a Los Angeles courthouse. It was a moment charged with anticipation and significance, as I was about to be sworn in as a newly minted American citizen. My heart swelled with a deep, profound pride as the words of allegiance rolled off my tongue. America, to me, symbolized the very essence of freedom and opportunity—the greatest country on earth.

This moment was not merely a formality; it was the culmination of a journey marked by sacrifice, courage, and unyielding hope. My family and I had traveled across continents, leaving behind everything we knew to chase a dream that seemed almost unreachable. The journey had been arduous and fraught with challenges, but every hardship was borne with the belief that perseverance would lead us to victory.

Our voyage had begun far from the shores of America. We left behind a familiar world, navigating through obstacles and uncertainties with the steadfast resolve that a new life in America would bring us the freedom and opportunities we had long yearned for. Each step of our journey was a testament to our determination and sacrifice—leaving behind family, friends, and the comfort of the known to embrace the promise of the unknown.

As I stood in that courthouse, the enormity of what we had achieved struck me. The pride I felt was not just for the personal achievement of becoming a citizen but for the fulfillment of a collective dream that my family had fought so hard to realize. This was a moment of triumph, validating the sacrifices made and the dreams we had nurtured.

My belief that perseverance could turn dreams into reality had been proven true. The trials we faced had only strengthened our resolve, and as I looked around at my fellow new citizens, I saw reflections of my own hopes and aspirations in their eyes. The ceremony was a powerful reminder of the promise that America held—a promise we had worked so diligently to attain. It was a milestone that reaffirmed my faith in the dream of freedom and opportunity, making it one of the proudest moments of my life.

HEALTH CHALLENGES AT SIXTEEN AND THIRTY-TWO

As a high school sophomore, I encountered a challenge I never anticipated: Bell's palsy. It began with subtle, unsettling changes—my lips drooping, my eyes struggling to open fully. I tried to hide these symptoms, but my mom noticed and took me to the doctor. The diagnosis was Bell's palsy, a virus affecting the seventh cranial nerve, and it hit me hard.

The news felt like a crushing weight. Already battling self-esteem issues, this condition amplified my insecurities. Every glance in the mirror was a reminder of how I felt different. I could sense the unease in my peers' eyes, and the fear of judgment loomed over me like a dark cloud. The daily routine of cortisone shots and eye drops was a constant reminder of my condition. At school, I felt like a spectacle, my attempts to blend in overshadowed by the fear of scrutiny. I recall overhearing whispers from classmates that felt like daggers. Their words cut deeper than I wanted to admit, leaving me with a profound sense of isolation.

Fortunately, after six weeks of intense treatment, the medication began to work, and I made a full recovery. Life seemed to return to normal, but the relief was fleeting. Years later, at thirty-two, Bell's palsy struck again, this time with even greater intensity.

The second episode was a far graver ordeal. The recovery process dragged on, leaving me with permanent damage to my left eye. The emotional toll was profound; each day felt like an uphill battle against frustration and a growing sense of loss. I struggled to find a semblance of normalcy and grappled with feelings of helplessness. But in the midst of this struggle, I refused to let it define me. Instead, I discovered a wellspring of strength within myself. I learned to accept my imperfections and found solace in the resilience of the human spirit.

Throughout this challenging journey, the unwavering support of my mentors and loved ones became a beacon of hope. Their encouragement lifted me when I felt like giving up and reminded me of the strength I possessed. Today, I view my experience with Bell's palsy as a poignant reminder of life's fragility and the enduring power of perseverance. It taught me to cherish the simple joys, like the ability to smile or blink without difficulty, and deepened my empathy for those who face their own hidden struggles.

CANCER SURVIVOR (1984)

At thirty-five, my world was shattered once again with the devastating diagnosis of stage 3 uterine sarcoma. The words fell like a heavy stone, crushing the dreams I had nurtured for years. An emergency hysterectomy became my only option, stripping away not just the chance to have more children, but also a vital piece of my identity and the future I had envisioned.

From a young age, I had dreamt of a bustling household filled with the laughter of four children, a dream that seemed as natural and promising as the morning sun. I pictured a life surrounded by the joy of a large family, my home overflowing with love and noise. Instead, fate delivered a harsh reality. Though I was blessed with two beautiful daughters and seven precious grandchildren, the void left by the loss of my dream was profound and deep.

The pain of that loss was a raw, aching emptiness, a

wound that seemed impossible to heal. Every corner of my home, once filled with the anticipation of a larger family, now felt hollow and silent. Each day was a reminder of the dream that would never be, and the heartache cut through my soul like a relentless winter wind.

Yet, amidst the tears and the heartache, there was an unexpected source of solace and strength. My daughters and grandchildren became my sanctuary, their presence a gentle balm for my wounded spirit. Their laughter, like the softest music, became a melody that eased my sorrow. Their hugs were a refuge, a tangible reminder of the love that still surrounded me, even if it was different from what I had imagined.

In their eyes, I saw the love that transcended the dreams that were lost. They became my reason to smile, my beacon of hope in the darkest moments. Each shared moment, each embrace, was a testament to the love that existed beyond the confines of my shattered dreams.

Looking back, I see now that perhaps G-d's plan for me was beyond what I could have ever imagined. My journey, marked by love and resilience, has been shaped by a family that, while smaller in number, is immeasurable in the depth of its love. In the end, it was not the size of the family that defined its worth, but the strength of the love we shared.

A NEW CHAPTER IN THE SIERRA NEVADA FOOTHILLS (1980)

In 1980, my husband and I embraced a profound shift, trading the hustle and bustle of Huntington Beach, California, for a tranquil ten-acre ranch nestled in the Sierra Nevada Foothills. This new home became more than just a place to live; it became our sanctuary, where love and growth intertwined in every corner. Here, we raised our dynamic, beautiful daughters and joyfully welcomed our treasured grandchildren.

The land, with its majestic tall oak and pine trees, is not merely picturesque; it is a haven of serenity. Each morning, as I take in the breathtaking mountain views, I am enveloped in a profound sense of humility and gratitude, feeling deeply blessed.

This journey has come full circle, echoing the continuity of my life's story. I think back to the small, humble house in Israel, where a vibrant pomegranate tree grew, symbolizing joy and resilience through the trials of my childhood. In my current home, another flourishing pomegranate tree stands tall, mirroring the strength and spirit that have defined my life.

As our family gathers beneath its branches, we are enveloped in the warmth of our shared history and the strength we have drawn from overcoming challenges. The pomegranate tree is more than just a plant; it is a living link to our roots and a vivid reminder of our enduring perseverance. In the Torah, the pomegranate is esteemed for its 613 seeds, representing good deeds and the fullness of life. Our tree, standing as a testament to the fruitfulness of our journey, symbolizes the abundant blessings we cherish and the unyielding strength that has guided us through the years.

A LEGACY OF FAITH

In the heart of Grass Valley, California, my husband and I embarked on a pioneering journey, driven by a vision of community and continuity. We became the founding members of the Jewish Community Center, a beacon of faith and tradition in a region that had long yearned for such a sanctuary. Our commitment to this endeavor was steadfast; we co-signed as grantors to ensure that our community would have a synagogue—a sacred space where our shared faith could take root and flourish. We opened our home for countless holiday celebrations and fundraisers, welcoming friends and neighbors with open arms, creating a strong sense of warmth and unity.

This synagogue soon became the heart of our community, a vibrant center where Judaism could be practiced, celebrated, and passed down through generations. I vividly remember the profound moment when every seat in the sanctuary was filled for my daughter Courtney's bat mitzvah. It was a historic occasion, as she became the first to be confirmed in over a century, reading from the Torah with grace and confidence that brought tears of joy to many eyes. Her Bat Mitzvah was not just a personal milestone but a symbol of hope and continuity, paving the way for future generations within our community to stand proudly before the Torah.

In our family alone, the legacy of faith has been carried forward with deep reverence. My grandchildren—Michael, Lila Star, Charles Elijah, and Carter Gabriel—each stood before the Torah for their Bar and Bat Mitzvahs, continuing a tradition that we had worked so hard to establish. These moments were not merely ceremonies; they were affirmations of a heritage that binds us together across generations.

The creation of this synagogue has allowed us to fulfill the cherished principle of "l'dor v'dor," passing our traditions from generation to generation. Our synagogue stands as a testament to this enduring legacy. The walls, filled with the echoes of prayers and songs, are a reminder of our collective efforts to preserve and nurture our culture. Every Shabbat service, every holiday celebration, and every Torah reading brings together the stories of those who came before us with the hopes and dreams of those who will follow.

Through this sacred space, we have created a haven where the values of our faith are not only preserved but thrive. It has become a place where young and old come together to celebrate our shared heritage, where each generation finds strength and solace in the continuity of our traditions. Our legacy is etched in the roots of the community we have built— a community that honors the past while embracing the future, ensuring that the light of Judaism continues to shine brightly for generations to come.

REFLECTING ON LIFE'S BLESSINGS

Our life in the Sierra Nevada Foothills is a haven of serenity and joy, surrounded by the splendor of nature and the warmth of family. As I sit by the fire pit in our backyard, the crackling flames dance against the backdrop of a breathtaking mountain view. Each flicker of the fire illuminates the faces of our loved ones gathered around, their laughter mingling with the gentle rustling of leaves in the evening breeze. The sky above is a canvas of twilight hues—deep blues and soft pinks that gradually fade into the tranquil darkness, with the first stars beginning to twinkle.

The lush green grass stretches out like a soft, inviting carpet beneath our feet, and the vibrant colors of the rose garden burst forth in a glorious display of reds, pinks, and yellows. Their delicate petals, kissed by the afternoon sun, release a subtle, sweet fragrance that fills the air, enhancing the peaceful ambiance of our outdoor sanctuary. Nearby, the gentle sound of water trickling from the fountains provides a soothing melody, harmonizing with the natural symphony of birdsong and the distant call of wildlife.

As I REFLECT ON THE JOURNEY THAT BROUGHT ME HERE, I AM overwhelmed with a profound sense of gratitude. Each challenge faced and triumph celebrated has shaped the rich and rewarding life I now enjoy. The journey has been marked by moments of struggle and joy, resilience and growth. Every twist and turn has been a step toward this place of peace and contentment, where the beauty of nature and the love of family converge.

Looking out over the mountain vista from our backyard, I

am reminded of the resilience that has shaped my path. The rugged peaks and verdant valleys are a metaphor for the strength and endurance that have carried me through life's ups and downs. The tranquil setting is not just a backdrop but a reflection of the inner calm and fulfillment I feel.

As I sit by the fire, surrounded by the beauty of our garden and the comforting presence of loved ones, I am filled with hope and anticipation for the future. The glow of the fire, the gentle flow of water, and the vibrant colors of the roses are not just elements of our landscape—they are symbols of the life we have built and the memories we continue to create. The future beckons with promise, and I face it with a heart full of optimism, knowing that the best is yet to come.

HUNTINGTON BEACH (1989)

In 1989, a pivotal moment unfolded in our lives: my husband's company was sold. This wasn't just a business transaction; it was a testament to his relentless commitment and the countless hours he devoted to providing for our family. The sale marked the beginning of a new chapter, one that opened doors to opportunities beyond my wildest dreams. I am profoundly grateful for the blessings we have received from G-d and our family, feeling a deep sense of humility and awe at the journey that has led us here.

At forty-two, my husband retired as a successful entrepreneur, but his spirit of innovation and drive didn't wane. He embarked on establishing a new company, one that continues to thrive and inspire. His unwavering determination is a constant source of motivation for me, a reminder of the heights we can reach through hard work and vision.

Reflecting on my own journey from modest beginnings, I am reminded of the importance of cherishing every gift and blessing. Life has taught me not to take anything for granted.

While I don't indulge in extravagance, I find profound joy in spoiling my grandchildren. In a world often prone to excess, I derive pleasure from discovering unique treasures—pieces of furniture, jewelry, and art—that bring beauty and history into our lives. Each item is a reminder of the richness and depth of our experiences.

Through social media, I connect with family and friends around the globe, sharing glimpses of a life that might seem idyllic in pictures. But I know that perfection is an illusion; life is about what we make of it, and I choose to stay positive. Surrounded by loving and supportive friends, I've learned to distinguish between genuine relationships and those that are superficial. My friendships are built on mutual respect and reciprocity, and I steer clear of those who don't share these values. This journey of personal growth has shaped me into the person I am today.

The greatest joy in my life comes from being a wife, mother, grandmother, and a cherished friend. My heart swells with happiness as I think of the adventures I've had and the precious moments spent with my seven grandchildren. Exploring faraway lands with them, watching their eyes light up with wonder, and sharing stories and experiences are among my most treasured memories. I hope to inspire them to approach the world with curiosity and awe, just as I have.

I believe deeply in the power of manifestation and the importance of believing in our dreams. We shape our future by nurturing our desires and acting upon our beliefs. It's a reminder that our dreams are the seeds of our future reality. Each day, I strive to overcome the self-doubt that sometimes tells me I'm unworthy of the abundance G-d has bestowed upon me. I am dedicated to my work, not to impress others, but to fulfill my own sense of purpose.

The poignant words of the late singer Nightbird resonate with me deeply: "You can't wait until life isn't hard anymore until you decide to be happy." These words remind me to find joy amidst life's struggles and challenges. True happiness comes from within, and I am determined to embrace it fully, no matter the obstacles I face.

Every challenge, every setback is an opportunity for growth and resilience. I aspire to empower myself and others by simplifying and making effectiveness effortless. I greet each day with gratitude, embracing mistakes as part of the journey and viewing others with understanding. I value a community that offers honest feedback, whether it's good or bad, as it helps me grow.

Building my confidence, cherishing time with my daughter and grandchildren, and making a positive impact on others are my core goals. I aim to be a reliable friend, stay creative, and make a difference in the lives of those around me. As I go to sleep each night, I find solace in the belief that after every storm, there is peace and calm, making life's beauty all the more profound.

CHAPTER NINETEEN
REDISCOVERING ROOTS

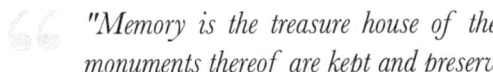

"Memory is the treasure house of the mind wherein the monuments thereof are kept and preserved."

— THOMAS FULLER

VISITING LOS ANGELES

I n the heart of Los Angeles, nestled within the Fairfax district, lies a neighborhood that cradles the echoes of my teenage years—years that have profoundly shaped my future in ways I never anticipated. Each time I drove through this vibrant area on my way to my mom's house, I couldn't resist taking a detour through my old neighborhood. It was a ritual that transported me back in time, to a world brimming with life and possibilities.

The Fairfax district was a lively Jewish community alive with the pulse of everyday joys. Across from our apartment lived a group of young musicians, their guitars strumming melodies that resonated deeply within me. They were Southern boys who introduced me to the soulful twang of country music, their tunes filling our street with an infectious sense of joy and freedom.

Those years were a celebration of diversity and artistic expression. The streets thrummed with the laughter of children and the vibrant strains of music drifting from open windows. It was in this dynamic environment that my dreams began to take root, guiding me toward the person I aspired to become and the path I was destined to follow.

Yet, among the many memories that I hold dear, one particular thread remained untangled—a lingering curiosity about the girl next door. She was a friend whose presence was as comforting as it was enigmatic. As the years rolled on, she seemed to have vanished without a trace. Five decades later, driven by a need for closure and an understanding of what had been lost, I decided to revisit my old neighborhood.

I parked my Mercedes Benz in the familiar driveway adjacent to the building and knocked on the door of her former apartment, my heart brimming with hope. However, the door was answered by a stranger—a woman who looked at me with a mixture of confusion and curiosity. Despite my attempts to reconnect and jog her memory, she could not recall the past I so vividly remembered. I felt a wave of disappointment and confusion wash over me, a realization that closure might remain elusive.

As I drove away, I came to terms with the fact that some chapters of our lives may remain unfinished. Yet, in that acceptance, I found a deep sense of solace. My journey had been one of resilience and determination, a testament to my ability to stay grounded and focused despite the challenges of my teenage years. Reflecting on the lessons learned, I felt a profound gratitude for the memories that shaped me.

Though my teenage years were marked by struggle, they were also the crucible in which my future was forged. They paved the way for a life rich with hope and opportunity, reminding me that our past, while it may hold unanswered questions, is also the foundation upon which we build our future.

A TRIP TO TUNISIA, NORTH AFRICA (1981)

In 1981, I set out on a journey that was as much about my mother's past as it was about rediscovering my own roots. We began with a flight to Djerba, a small island south of Tunisia, steeped in the sacred echoes of a bygone era. This island, once a vibrant center of worship and celebration for thousands of Jews, including my mother's family, felt like a sacred tapestry woven with history and faith. As we landed, the weight of centuries seemed to press down on us, a palpable reminder of the times of King Solomon.

A week later, our journey took us to Tunis, the capital city, where my mother's childhood memories lay hidden among the streets. Walking through those old avenues was an emotional pilgrimage, every corner echoing with the ghosts of her past. The Jewish synagogue, once a beacon of community, was now boarded up and silent. Her old school, once a bustling center of learning, had vanished into memory. We roamed through the narrow streets, navigating through bustling tunnels alive with merchants, until we finally stumbled upon her old street.

The moment we emerged into "Avenue of the Doctor," the heart of the city seemed to hold its breath. My mother's face, lit with a mixture of nostalgia and sadness, was a vivid testament to the passage of time. We arrived at a large, empty courtyard, the scene of countless childhood adventures now swallowed by silence. It was then that I saw her standing beside a pile of rubble—fragmented, colored mosaic tiles from the building of her childhood, demolished only a month earlier.

The sight of my mother, tears streaming down her face, was heart-wrenching. Here she was, confronting the remnants of the home where she had spent her formative years. She spoke of climbing up to the terrace rooftop, of the terror she felt during the war and the Nazi occupation. In that moment, we embraced tightly, the weight of our shared grief palpable. We prayed for those who had been lost simply because they were Jewish. Whispering softly, I assured her, "It's okay, Mom. You are safe now."

I picked up one of the broken tiles, its ornate patterns now a jumbled mosaic of a world gone by. I studied it, pondering the stories it might tell—of family gatherings, joyous celebrations, and the everyday miracles of life that now seemed distant and fragile. That broken tile now occupies a place of honor in my home, a poignant symbol of our shared history and enduring spirit. It's a constant reminder of where we came from, who we are now, and the path we continue to forge.

This journey was more than a mere trip; it was a deep dive into the essence of our heritage. It taught me that while the past shapes us, it does not confine us. The legacy we inherit is one of strength, courage, and resilience. As I reflect on this experience, my heart swells with a profound sense of gratitude for my mother's unyielding strength and courage. I am reminded of the importance of honoring our past while bravely stepping into the future.

Returning home, I carried with me the weight of history and the realization of the trials my mother and her family had endured. Yet, there was also a profound gratitude for the life they had built despite overwhelming adversity. Their resilience and strength are a beacon to me, and I vowed to carry their stories forward with pride, ensuring that their legacy endures for generations to come.

CHAPTER TWENTY

LOVE CREATES STRENGTH -
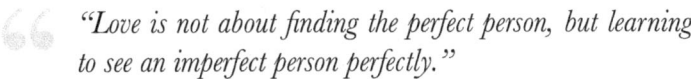 אהבה עושה חיל

> *"Love is not about finding the perfect person, but learning to see an imperfect person perfectly."*
>
> — *SAM KEEN*

A BLIND DATE - 1973

During a time of dreams and aspirations, I longed for a place to call my own—a sanctuary where I could build my future. Weekends were spent driving around, visiting rentals, and searching for that perfect place. One day, I stumbled upon it—a beautiful, newly built studio apartment that seemed like the ideal haven. But when I discovered the rent, my heart sank; it was far beyond my means.

In my moment of despair, I turned to my dear friend and mentor Dina Bar El, a renowned clothing designer who had become like a surrogate older sister to me. Dina, who always had my back, suggested I meet her boyfriend's older brother, convinced we would hit it off. Despite my busy schedule, I took a leap of faith and agreed to meet him.

Blind Date

When I rang the doorbell of his home, I was met with a warm, inviting smile that seemed to light up the room. He radiated kindness and charm, and as we talked, I found him incredibly engaging and intelligent. Our first date at Marina Del Rey in Santa Monica was enchanting—over drinks and laughter, I discovered a connection I had never felt before.

As our relationship deepened, I had the chance to meet his family. Unfortunately, what I encountered was far from welcoming. His father, a successful real estate broker, was known for his complicated personal life, while his mother, a spoiled and calculating figure, cast a shadow over our growing bond. She disparaged me with hurtful remarks, calling me the "dirty Israeli," and questioned my worth.

Despite their disapproval, our love flourished. We built a life together, creating a family that became my sanctuary. We faced challenges with unwavering support for each other, and as his mother's negativity drove a wedge between us, we made the heart-wrenching decision to step away from her presence.

Her passing was a solemn occasion, marked by the absence of mourning. Yet, this somber moment underscored the profound importance of the love and family we had built. Amidst the heartache, I found solace in the embrace of our daughters and grandchildren. The family we created became my greatest treasure, a testament to resilience and unconditional love.

In the quiet moments, I reflect on the journey that brought us here—full of trials, yet rich with the beauty of connection and family. It is this love, found against the odds, that fills my heart with gratitude. The joy and warmth we share bring tears of happiness to my eyes, reminding me of the strength we draw from one another and the love that defines our lives.

This story is a celebration of the bonds we forge, the family we create, and the love that guides us through life's trials. It's a testament to the beauty of finding home in the hearts of those we cherish.

SEPTEMBER 1975

Jeffrey and I stood side by side, our hearts racing as we faced the judge in the bustling Los Angeles County courthouse—the very same place where I had first become an American citizen. At precisely 10:10 a.m., the room seemed to hold its breath as we exchanged vows in a simple yet profound civil ceremony. I, a hopeful twenty-three-year-old, and Jeff, my steadfast twenty-seven-year-old love, clasped hands tightly, his fingers intertwining with mine in a perfect embrace.

Earlier that morning, Jeff had surprised me with two dozen radiant red roses from the downtown flower market. The sweet gesture filled me with happiness so profound that it felt like my heart might burst. I held the bouquets in my left hand, their fragrance mingling with the nervous excitement that hung in the air.

As we pledged our love and commitment, I couldn't help but reflect on our journey—a rollercoaster ride that had brought us to this moment. Each year, on our anniversary, I pull out my vintage rayon floral skirt and blouse, while Jeff dons his beige suit, and we reminisce about the adventures and challenges that shaped our lives. From family dramas to joyous milestones, every moment has been a testament to our enduring bond.

Our story began just six months before that fateful day when we, two young souls who had unexpectedly found love, embarked on a journey neither of us could have predicted. We faced moments of family strife, shared the sheer joy of building a life together, and weathered heartbreaking losses that deepened our appreciation for one another.

Together, we traveled the world, each adventure adding to the rich tapestry of our shared history. We welcomed two beautiful daughters into our lives, who in turn blessed us with seven lively and loving grandchildren. These precious souls fill our home with laughter and light, a constant reminder of the love that has anchored us through thick and thin.

As I gazed into Jeff's eyes that day, I knew that our love was something truly special—a story of resilience, unwavering commitment, and a bond that grew stronger with each passing year. Leaving the courthouse hand in hand, I was filled with immense gratitude for the incredible journey we had shared and the countless adventures yet to come.

Jeff and I are opposites that complement each other in the most beautiful way. We are two independent individuals who honor and respect each other's personal growth by honoring our marriage. Jeff embodies simplicity, preferring to stay out of the limelight and shine it on others, while I thrive on building deep, meaningful connections. His effortless kindness, warmth, and ability to listen make him a comforting presence for those around him.

I, on the other hand, am fiercely protective of our family. My nurturing spirit, while sometimes seen as spoiling, is a way to show how cherished and supported our loved ones are. Our home is a haven of laughter and love, grounded in the belief that generosity and respect for everyone are what make us better human beings.

Our journey together has not only been about the love we share but also about the values we stand for. We believe in a world where love and acceptance reign supreme, where everyone is treated with dignity and kindness. As we look back on our life together, we are proud of our family and the values we hold dear. Our story is one of love, compassion, and a profound respect for humanity.

My Daughters

Traveling has been more than just sightseeing; it has been about sharing experiences with our daughters and grandchildren, showing them the endless possibilities that await those who dare to dream. Watching their eyes light up with wonder and their hearts expand with each new discovery is a gift we treasure deeply.

Nestled in the foothills of the California Sierra Nevada's, we have created a life that is as beautiful as it is fulfilling. When asked about the secret to our long and happy marriage, we always say it is by the grace of G-d. We believe that He brought us together, two souls from different continents and backgrounds, at the perfect moment. Our love, guided by His hand, has remained unwavering.

Laughter has been the cornerstone of our relationship, along with a deep mutual respect that has carried us through the good times and the bad. We have never given up on each other or our dreams, always looking forward to what the future holds while cherishing the present.

As we approach our fiftieth year of marriage, I am reminded of the moment I first met Jeff and knew he was the one I wanted to share my life with. It was as if G-d had placed us on this earth to be each other's everything, and I am grateful every day for the love and partnership we share.

Our hope is that our children and grandchildren will find a love as deep and enduring as ours, knowing that with faith, laughter, and unwavering support, anything is possible.

CHAPTER TWENTY-ONE

A NEW BEGINNING

 "The greatest glory in living lies not in never falling, but in rising every time we fall."

— *NELSON MANDELA*

ROOTS AND REFLECTIONS

As I reflect on the journey of my life, I am reminded of the roots of a pomegranate tree, deeply embedded in the soil of my past, nurturing the growth of my present. My story is intricately woven with the stories of my family—tales of resilience and courage passed down through generations. These stories have anchored me, shaping who I am and providing the strength to face life's challenges.

Growing up in Israel, I was immersed in a culture rich in history and tradition. Each day presented lessons in resilience as I navigated childhood, drawing strength from the deep roots of my heritage. When my family moved to Italy, I embraced the opportunity to explore new horizons, learning to adapt to new customs and ways of life.

The transition to America marked a new chapter, filled with both excitement and uncertainty. Facing the complexities of adolescence in a new land, I discovered the true power of resilience, relying on the lessons of my past to guide me through the present. Through it all, I remained steadfast in my belief that no matter the obstacles, I had the inner strength to overcome them.

Now, as I write the final chapters of my memoir, I realize that my story extends beyond myself. It is a narrative of resilience, overcoming adversity, and embracing the journey that has shaped me. In sharing my story, I hope to inspire others to embrace their own paths, knowing that they too possess the strength to face their challenges.

Looking back on the roots of my pomegranate tree, I am filled with gratitude for the stories that have shaped me and the resilience that has carried me through. My story is a testament to the enduring power of resilience—a reminder that no matter where life takes us, our roots will always sustain us, guiding us toward a future filled with promise and possibility.

As we part ways, I thank you for joining me on this journey through the roots of my pomegranate tree, for listening to my story so it is not lost in the relentless march of time. I hope these tales have left a lasting imprint on your heart, much like the intricate patterns of light filtering through the leaves of a tree, casting shadows that dance with the rhythm of life.

May you carry with you the essence of my journey—the

essence of resilience and strength that has sustained me through the seasons of my life. And as you continue on your own path, may you find inspiration in the stories of the past and may they guide you toward a future filled with hope, courage, and an unwavering belief in the power of the human spirit.

A JOURNEY OF SELF-DISCOVERY

ALIZA ELLINS

Throughout my early years and into young adulthood, I grappled with weight—a continuous cycle of gaining and losing. Eventually, I gained clarity about the root causes of these struggles and made a conscious effort to transform my relationship with food and embrace a healthier lifestyle.

In 2023, I lost forty-five pounds and dropped four dress sizes—a journey I proudly share on social media to inspire others. It hasn't been easy; there were moments of struggle and doubt. Yet, I persevered, knowing that my physical and mental health were worth the effort.To boost my confidence and happiness, I surrounded myself with dynamic, like-minded friends and engaged in activities that nurtured my growth. I planted an organic vegetable and rose garden, finding joy in nurturing life and beauty. Most importantly, I created a loving family, watching them flourish and become the best versions of themselves.

Daily meditation has been transformative, helping me to be more mindful and grateful for the blessings in my life. It has taught me to be purposeful, reducing stress and allowing me to stay focused and calm.

I believe access to healthcare and education on healthy choices is crucial. The alarming obesity rates in America highlight the need for better education and resources to promote healthier lifestyles.

My wish for everyone is to find success and stay grounded, surrounded by positive, loving, and supportive people who accept you for who you are. I've learned to give myself grace when I falter and to return to my journey with renewed determination. Life is about continuous growth and improvement, and I am committed to becoming the best version of myself every day.

ACKNOWLEDGMENTS

While writing this book, I took time to reflect on all the people who have helped me become who I am today. Over the past seven decades, there are countless individuals I could thank, but I would like to take a moment to express my deepest gratitude to those who have inspired and taught me every day.

Yvette Neyer, my Big Sister from the Big Sister and Big Brother Organization, has been a trusted mentor and friend since 1969. Your guidance and love left an indelible mark on my life.

Jeffrey Ellins, the love of my life since 1975, thank you for being my partner through all the ups and downs, and for supporting me as I pursued my goals and dreams. Your unwavering support has been my greatest strength.

Dina Bar El, a role model since 1973, thank you for being someone I could always count on during some of the most challenging times of my life. Your friendship has been a beacon of light.

Sherri Hunt Todd, a mentor from 1975, thank you for imparting your leadership skills and helping me navigate my role in the banking industry. Your guidance enabled me to help others reach their greatest potential.

Stephanie Olivolo, my eldest daughter, thank you for keeping life fun and exciting and for challenging me to be a better version of myself. Your love and the gift of three beautiful, loving grandchildren—Michael, Paris, and Mason—have filled my life with endless happiness.

Courtney Morgan, my youngest daughter, thank you for your unwavering love, support, and generosity. You have blessed me with four wonderful grandchildren—Makayla, Elijah, Gabriel, and Lila Star—who bring immeasurable joy to my life.

I want to give a special thanks to my grandchildren Michael Ellins and Lila Star Morgan who played a crucial role in making this book a reality. Their valuable input, collaborative editing, and dedication to this project have been a true labor of love. I am deeply grateful for their help and proud to have had them by my side throughout this journey.

To all of you, thank you from the bottom of my heart for being a part of my life and for helping me tell my story. Your love, support, and inspiration have made this book possible, and I am forever thankful.

ABOUT THE AUTHOR

Aliza Ellins, an Israeli born writer, emerged as a beacon of resilience in the face of adversity. The eldest among sixteen siblings, raised by a single mom, she navigated a challenging childhood marked by the struggles of experiencing homelessness, being a latchkey child, sexual victimization, and poverty within a multigenerational family dynamic.

Aliza's journey took her across continents, ultimately finding stability and a new beginning in the United States. Her positive attitude, and continual perseverance, Aliza transformed her hardships into stepping stones to success.

Rising as a prominent business entrepreneur, she not only achieved professional success but also built a loving and beautiful family.

www.ingramcontent.com/pod-product-compliance
Lightning Source LLC
Chambersburg PA
CBHW060532130626
46553CB00002B/723

* 9 7 9 8 9 9 1 2 1 9 7 2 3 *